Occupational Pension Schemes 1987

Eighth Survey by the Government Actuary

London:HMSO

ISBN 0 11 701225 4

Contents

Acknowledgements

The Government Actuary acknowledges support for making the survey and assistance generally from the Confederation of British Industry, the Trades Union Congress, the National Association of Pension Funds, the Association of British Insurers, the Association of Consulting Actuaries, the Society of Pension Consultants, and the Institute of Actuaries and the Faculty of Actuaries; but is particularly grateful to the employers who co-operated by completing the questionnaires. Thanks are also due to the organising staff, interviewers and respondents of the government's General Household Survey for providing both the comprehensive sampling frame of employers used in the survey and information on the extent of the rights of individuals to occupational pension scheme benefits.

1 Introduction and Summary of Main Findings

1.1 This is the eighth survey of occupational pension schemes made by the Government Actuary in a series which began in 1956 and has continued every fourth year since 1963. The surveys have determined the extent to which employees in the United Kingdom have been covered by occupational pension schemes and analysed the nature of the benefits provided, the amounts of income and expenditure of schemes and other matters of interest to the government, employers and employees. Each survey has been based on information obtained from a large and comprehensive sample of pension schemes.

1.2 The information in the current report is based in the first place on answers given by about 10,000 employees to the government's General Household Survey (GHS) in 1987 and, if they were members of schemes, on the answers to questionnaires addressed to their pension scheme managers or employers. The replies received have been rated up to give the best possible estimates for the UK as a whole, paying regard to other sources of statistics which are available. The methods of the survey are described in detail in Appendix A1 and the questionnaire forms are reproduced in Appendix A2, whilst Appendix A3 contains a glossary of the terms used in the report.

Membership

1.3 The survey shows that the number of employees in occupational pension schemes in respect of their current employment in the United Kingdom in 1987 was a little over 10½ million, or 49 per cent of all employees in employment (including those only working part-time) and the Armed Forces, as compared with the 52 per cent coverage indicated in the previous survey in 1983. The reduction is attributable to changes in the pattern of employment in Britain in recent years, rather than to conscious decisions of employers or employees. The number of pensions in payment reached 6 million, and, in addition, about 3½ million people had a right to a preserved pension on reaching pension age in respect of a former employment (of whom just over one million were also earning pensions rights in respect of their current employment), making a total of about 19 million people with pension rights.

Scheme funds

1.4   Of the 19 million people with pension rights, 14 million were in schemes where there was an accumulated fund from which pensions are paid. The funds had a market value of about £260 billion at the end of 1987. An indication of the rate of growth of funds during 1987, before allowing for changes in the market value of the assets held, is given by the excess of income over expenditure under schemes in the year, which totalled about £14 billion. The liabilities in respect of pensions for public servants are not, in general, funded, but the total value of all occupational pension scheme liabilities, funded or unfunded, has been estimated at about £400 billion at mid 1987 for the purpose of the wealth estimates published in *Inland Revenue Statistics 1990.*

Benefit rules

1.5   Nearly 90 per cent of the 10½ million members were contracted-out of the earnings-related additional pension under the state scheme, mostly with pensions based on 1/60th of their final salaries, or, in the public sector, a pension based on 1/80ths together with a lump sum on retirement. Of the 10 per cent of members of non-contracted-out schemes nearly two-thirds also had pensions based on final salary.

1.6   In the private sector a small proportion of schemes had started to equalise normal retirement ages for men and women by the time of the survey; some schemes moving towards 60 for both, others towards 65 for both. In most parts of the public sector the practice has always been to have equal retirement ages for men and women. Other trends noted suggest continued improvements in ill-health early retirement provision, including an increase in the number of people covered by separate Permanent Health Insurance schemes, improvements in the level of death in service benefits and the extension of widowers' pension benefits.

Pensions increases

1.7   In the private sector 84 per cent of the pensioners in 1987 were in schemes which had granted at least one increase in their pensions in payment during the years 1984 to 1986, with a very high proportion receiving annual increases. On average the increases, where granted, were broadly in line with inflation over this period, but there were wide variations between schemes. In the public sector increases have continued to follow closely the movements in the Retail Prices Index under the Pensions (Increase) Acts.

2　Membership of Schemes

2.1　The estimated number of members of occupational pension schemes in 1987 is 10.6 million, or just under half of the total number of employees in employment (both full-time and part-time) and the Armed Forces. The total is made up of 7.2 million men and 3.4 million women. The proportion of employees covered has remained close to 50 per cent since about 1965, as the following paragraphs explain. In addition there are now about 2.6 million others who, though they are not members of a scheme in respect of their current employment, expect to receive a pension in respect of a former employment when they reach retirement age.

Pension coverage since the war

2.2　Just before the Second World War there were only about 2½ million members of occupational pension schemes, or about 15 per cent of the work force, but during the 1950s and most of the 1960s the number of people in schemes grew rapidly to reach about half the number of employees in employment, at which level it has remained. Considering the public and private sectors separately, the private sector coverage peaked at the end of the 1960s and then fell to about 40 per cent as a result of fewer male manual workers being covered, and has remained at about this level ever since, although there was a small fall in the percentage covered between 1983 and 1987. The public sector has shown over a long period a gradual trend towards universal coverage, reaching 95 per cent coverage for those working full-time in 1983, but this percentage also fell slightly between 1983 and 1987. Table 2.1 shows the changes in the membership of pension schemes over the years. The numbers of members in the two sectors have been much affected by the transfer of enterprises between the public and private sectors: the major changes affecting the 1987 survey as compared with the previous survey were the re-classifications of British Telecom, British Gas, and British Airways, together involving the transfer of about 350,000 occupational pension scheme members, representing a high proportion of the total employees in these industries, from the public to the private sector. This change might have been expected to raise the number and proportion of scheme members in the private sector, but in the event both have fallen due to offsetting factors.

Year	Private sector		Public sector		Total members	Total employed	Percentage employed who are members		
	Men	Women	Men	Women			Men	Women	Total
1953	2.5	0.6	2.4	0.7	6.2	21.9	34	18	28
1956	3.5	0.8	2.9	0.8	8.0	22.7	43	21	35
1963	6.4	0.8	3.0	0.9	11.1	22.9	63	21	48
1967	6.8	1.3	3.1	1.0	12.2	23.2	66	28	53
1971	5.5	1.3	3.2	1.1	11.1	22.5	62	28	49
1975	4.9	1.1	3.7	1.7	11.4	23.1	63	30	49
1979	4.6	1.5	3.7	1.8	11.6	23.4	62	35	50
1983	4.4	1.4	3.4	1.9	11.1	21.1	64	37	52
1987	4.4	1.4	2.8	2.0	10.6	21.6	60	35	49

The table excludes employees who have some pension rights but are not accruing benefits in respect of current employment.

Sources for numbers of scheme members: For 1953 the report of the Phillips Committee; subsequently, surveys by the Government Actuary.

2.3   The rise in the total numbers employed between 1983 and 1987 was accompanied by a fall in the total number of members of occupational pension schemes. This fall was, however, confined to men; the number of women who were members of schemes remained at about 3⅓ million, the level which has applied since 1979. However, the proportions of men and women employees in occupational pension schemes both fell between 1983 and 1987. For women part of the explanation lies in a larger proportion only working part-time, but for both men and women the main explanation appears to lie in the changes in the pattern of employment in the United Kingdom which have been taking place over many years, particularly the increase in the number of smaller businesses, the reduction in the numbers employed in the largest enterprises and the switch from manufacturing to service industries. These factors are analysed in detail in the report *General Household Survey 1987.*

Analysis of coverage in 1987

2.4   Table 2.2 gives an analysis of scheme membership in 1987 by sector and sub-sector, together with the corresponding totals of employees in employment. Just under 40 per cent of employees employed in the private sector were members of schemes: about 50 per cent of men and 20 per cent of women. In the public sector 75 per cent were covered: 90 per cent of men and 60 per cent of women.

4

Table 2.2 Pension scheme coverage 1987, United Kingdom

millions

Sector	Men Employees	Men Members	Women Employees	Women Members	Total Employees	Total Members
Civil employment:						
Private sector	8.9	4.4	6.3	1.4	15.2	5.8
Public sector:						
Public corporations	0.8	0.8	0.2	0.1	1.0	0.9
Central government	0.6	0.6	1.4	1.1	2.0	1.7
Local authorities	1.4	1.1	1.7	0.8	3.1	1.9
Total public sector	2.8	2.5	3.3	2.0	6.1	4.5
Total civilians	11.7	6.9	9.6	3.4	21.3	10.3
HM Forces:						
Central government	0.3	0.3	—	—	0.3	0.3
Totals	12.0	7.2	9.6	3.4	21.6	10.6

Employees are single counted—ie those with two jobs are counted once only.

2.5 Table 2.3 shows scheme members according to whether they are contracted-out of the earnings-related additional pension of the state scheme. The proportions contracted-out have remained at nearly 80 per cent for the private sector and 100 per cent for public sector.

Table 2.3 Pension scheme membership 1987 and whether contracted-out (C-out) or not contracted-out (Not c-out), United Kingdom

millions

Sector	Men Not C-out	Men c-out	Men Total	Women Not C-out	Women c-out	Women Total	Total Not C-out	Total c-out	Total Total
Private	3.4	1.0	4.4	1.1	0.3	1.4	4.5	1.3	5.8
Public	2.8	—	2.8	2.0	—	2.0	4.8	—	4.8
Totals	6.2	1.0	7.2	3.1	0.3	3.4	9.3	1.3	10.6

Table 2.4 Pension scheme coverage for full- and part-time employees

percentages

Civilian or HM Forces and sector	Men		Women		Total	
	Full-time	Part-time	Full-time	Part-time	Full-time	Part-time
Civil employment:						
Private sector	51	7	34	7	47	7
Public sector	92	12	91	21	91	21
Total civilians	61	8	55	12	59	11
HM Forces:						
Public sector	98	—	98	—	98	—
All employees	62	8	57	12	60	11

2.6   Table 2.4 shows pension scheme coverage separately for full- and part-time employees. The proportions for male part-time employees should be treated with caution as the estimate of the numbers in schemes is based on very small numbers in the sample; also a significant proportion of men working part-time will be over pension age. Further particulars for part-time employees are given in Table 2.8.

Private sector

2.7   Employees in the private sector are those employed by companies and unincorporated businesses and by non-profit-making bodies serving companies and individuals which are not subject to direct government control. The latter include bodies of a quasi-public nature such as universities. Self-employed persons are not included in the survey although many of them are paying premiums under retirement annuity policies with insurance companies, as are some employees who are not members of an occupational scheme. The publication *Inland Revenue Statistics 1989* shows that retirement annuity tax relief was allowed in 1.3 million cases in the year 1986-87, a substantial increase over the 0.7 million cases in 1982-83, the latest figure available at the time of the previous survey.

2.8   Table 2.5 shows that for full-time employees the likelihood of an employee being a member of a scheme increases with the size of establishment;

the general pattern shows little change from the previous survey apart from a further increase in the coverage for the largest establishments.

2.9   Pension scheme coverage varies little between different industries in the public sector, but in the private sector there are wide differences. Information on this appears in the report *General Household Survey 1987*. It is the industries which tend to have the smaller firms which have the lowest coverage.

Table 2.5 Coverage according to size of establishment; private sector, full-time employees

thousands

Size of establishment	Employees	Members	Non-members	Percentage of members
Number of employees				
1,2	390	80	310	21
3-24	3,590	890	2,700	25
25-99	2,990	1,270	1,720	42
100-999	3,680	2,290	1,390	62
1,000 and over	1,250	1,040	210	83
Totals	11,900	5,570	6,330	47

Public sector

2.10   The public sector comprises the public corporations and the government sector, which covers central and local government employees and the Armed Forces. Bodies which are in receipt of government grants, but which also have other appreciable means of financial support, for example the universities, are treated as being in the private sector. Full definitions are given in the glossary (Appendix A3).

Public corporations

2.11   In 1987 about 1 million employees were employed by public corporations. There were well over 50 of these statutory bodies. They include the nationalized industries, which at that time comprised the Post Office, coal mining, railways, steel, shipbuilding, electricity, buses, waterways and airports, and the other corporations. Particulars of pension coverage are given in Table 2.6. The other public corporations include the Bank of England, the broadcasting authorities, boards serving Northern Ireland, and a number of groups of bodies (each counted as a single scheme for the purposes of Table 2.6) such as the passenger transport executives. There were substantial falls in the numbers employed in public corporations between 1983 and 1987, because of privatisations of several nationalized industries and the deregulation of the bus services of the passenger transport executives, leaving just the small non-operational parts.

Table 2.6 Public corporations pension coverage

Employer	Number of schemes	Number of employees	Number of members	Percentage coverage
		thousands	thousands	%
Nationalized industries	20	870	815	94
Other public corporations	20	125	110	88
Totals	40	995	925	93

Government sector

2.12   Particulars of the composition and pension coverage of the government sector are shown in Table 2.7. The fact that only five-sixths of the teachers are members of pension schemes is attributable to the large number who are employed part-time, for example at evening classes, and are otherwise engaged in the service of other employers, or are working on their own account. The relatively low pension coverage of the general Local Government Superannuation Scheme and the National Health Service is also due to the large number of part-time employees. On the other hand, non-regular police officers and firemen have not been included with the regular officers as employees, although they are sometimes described as part-time employees, and hence the police and fire services appear in the table as having complete coverage.

Table 2.7 Central and local government pension coverage

Employer	Number of different arrangements	Number of employees	Number of members	Coverage
		thousands	thousands	%
Central government:				
HM Forces	1	320	320	100
Civil Service and other				
central government bodies	15	775	730	94
Health authorities	1	1,210	925	76
Local authorities:				
Lecturers and teachers	1	735	600	82
Police officers (regular)	1	135	135	100
Firemen (regular)	1	40	40	100
Other employees of local				
authorities	2	2,145	1,140	53
Totals	22	5,360	3,890	73

Part-time employees

2.13   Just over a tenth of employees who work part-time are members of occupational pension schemes. Further details are given in Table 2.8. The qualifications in regard to the figures for men mentioned in paragraph 2.6 apply here also.

Table 2.8 Part-time employees pension scheme coverage

thousands

Sector	Men		Women		Total	
	Employees	Members	Employees	Members	Employees	Members
Private sector	400	30	2,900	200	3,300	230
Public sector	100	10	1,400	300	1,500	310
Totals	500	40	4,300	500	4,800	540

Eligibility for membership

2.14   Further information about eligibility conditions for membership and the reasons why employees are not in pension schemes is given in Chapter 5, from paragraph 5.12 onwards.

Preserved benefits

2.15   In 1987 about 3.5 million people of working age had a right to a preserved pension in respect of employment which they had previously left, payable at their normal retirement age. Further details are given in Chapter 11.

3 Pensioners

Numbers of pensioners

3.1   The number of pensions in payment from occupational schemes in 1987 is estimated to have been about 6 million. The numbers of pensioners grew rapidly in the early 1980s, in both the private and public sectors, as schemes became more mature and the large generation born in the years immediately after the First World War came up to retirement age. Details are shown in Table 3.1.

Table 3.1 Numbers of pensions in payment 1953-1987: United Kingdom

millions

Year	Private sector		Public sector		Total
	Former employees	Widows and other dependants	Former employees	Widows and other dependants	
1953	0.2	—	0.6	0.1	0.9
1956	0.3	—	0.7	0.1	1.1
1963	0.6	0.1	0.9	0.2	1.8
1967	0.8	0.2	1.1	0.2	2.3
1971	1.1	0.2	1.3	0.3	2.9
1975	1.1	0.2	1.7	0.4	3.4
1979	1.2	0.2	1.8	0.5	3.7
1983	1.8	0.3	2.2	0.7	5.0
1987	2.3	0.6	2.4	0.7	6.0

Sources: For 1953 the Report of the Phillips Committee; subsequently, surveys by the Government Actuary.

3.2   Table 3.2 shows the numbers of pensioners in 1987 according to the sector, and whether they were male or female ex-employees or the surviving dependants of ex-employees. Strictly speaking these are numbers of pensions, rather than pensioners, but it is thought that the number of pensioners with pensions from more than one source is still relatively small and there is an offset in the number of unreported pensions paid from schemes with no current members.

Table 3.2 Numbers of pensions in payment 1987

millions

	Former employees		Widows and other dependants	Total
	Men	Women		
Private sector	1.6	0.7	0.6	2.9
Public sector:				
Public corporations	0.6	0.05	0.25	0.9
Central government	0.6	0.35	0.3	1.25
Local authorities	0.5	0.3	0.15	0.95
Totals, public sector	1.7	0.7	0.7	3.1
Totals, both sectors	3.3	1.4	1.3	6.0

4   Income and Expenditure of Schemes

4.1   Although the primary purpose of the survey is to obtain information about the nature and coverage of occupational schemes, it was decided that because of the limitations of the financial information which is available from other sources, the opportunity should again be taken to obtain some information about schemes' income and expenditure and the amount of funds held. On the present occasion such data were not requested in the main questionnaire but a separate single page supplementary questionnaire was sent to employers some months later. In this way financial information was obtained covering over 90 per cent of the membership of schemes for which the main questionnaire had been completed, as well as information about a further 77 schemes for which a main questionnaire had not been completed.

4.2   The object was to obtain accounting data for the calendar year 1987 but schemes were asked only to supply information in respect of the accounting period falling predominantly within that year. Where the accounting period did not coincide with the calendar year, the data were adjusted in order to obtain estimates for the calendar year.

4.3   Estimates of the income and expenditure of schemes in 1987, with corresponding figures for 1983, are shown in Table 4.1. The figures for 1983 incorporate some revisions to the estimated expenditure on lump sum benefits on death and retirement since the report on the previous survey. For benefits funded through insurance companies, the amount of the attributable investment income will not normally be available to the scheme and an estimate is included in the figure for rents, dividends and interest shown in the table, derived from the estimate of the funds held by insurance companies against their group scheme liabilities. (See paragraph 4.7 below). Also, a notional figure for the expenses of insurance companies in respect of insured schemes business has been included, solely to provide an approximate total figure for expenditure. The expenses for non-insured schemes are the amounts included in scheme accounts and will understate the costs of administering schemes which are often wholly or partially borne by employers. Capital appreciation on investments,

Table 4.1 Estimates of income and expenditure of pension schemes 1983 and 1987

£ million

	1983			1987		
	Private sector	Public sector	Total	Private sector	Public sector	Total
Income:						
Employers' contributions	6,200	5,700	11,900	6,650	7,600	14,250
Members' contributions (including additional voluntary contributions)	1,750	2,200	3,950	2,400	2,550	4,950
Transfer payments from other pension schemes	350	200	550	1,550	500	2,050
Rents, dividends and interest	5,200	2,350	7,550	10,550	3,450	14,000
Miscellaneous income	50	100	150	350	150	500
Total income	13,550	10,550	24,100	21,500	14,250	35,750
Expenditure:						
Pensions to former employees	2,100	4,400	6,500	4,550	7,200	11,750
Pensions to dependants of former employees	250	500	750	600	850	1,450
Lump sums on death	300	150	450	350	200	550
Lump sums on retirement	1,150	1,500	2,650	1,450	1,950	3,400
Transfer payments to other pension schemes or arrangements	350	200	550	1,800	650	2,450
Refunds of contributions to members	100	100	200	150	100	250
State scheme premiums	200	100	300	250	150	400
Expenses and miscellaneous expenditure	300	50	350	1,050	50	1,100
Total expenditure	4,750	7,000	11,750	10,200	11,150	21,350
Excess of income over expenditure	8,800	3,550	12,350	11,300	3,100	14,400
						millions
Numbers of active members	*5.8*	*5.3*	*11.1*	*5.8*	*4.8*	*10.6*
Numbers of pensioners	*2.1*	*2.9*	*5.0*	*2.9*	*3.1*	*6.0*

14

whether realized or unrealized, is not included in the table. In making comparisons between the figures for the private and public sectors the inclusion in the figures for the public sector of the unfunded public service schemes, on the basis described in paragraph 4.6 below, should be borne in mind. Also in considering the changes since 1983 allowance must be made for the switch of some major schemes from the public to the private sector as a result of privatisations.

4.4   Table 4.1 shows that between 1983 and 1987 in the aggregate the income of schemes increased by 50 per cent, but expenditure increased by over 80 per cent. By comparison, the increase in the gross domestic product between those years was about 37 per cent, with a similar increase in average earnings. The more rapid growth of expenditure than of income reflects the gradual maturing of pension schemes, including an increase in the number of pensioners relative to the number of active members. A contributory factor to the relatively slower growth of income was the low growth in employers' contributions over the four year period. This is likely to have resulted from the surpluses generally revealed by actuarial valuations of schemes during this period, reflecting the high real rate of return secured on investments during most of the 1980s. One use of these surpluses has been to reduce the rates of employers' contributions where, as is often the case, employers meet the balance of the cost of a scheme.

4.5   A feature of Table 4.1 is the large growth in the amount of transfer payments compared with 1983. A relevant factor here is the changes in legislation in regard to preserved benefits and the provisions for transfer values. The totals also include significant amounts relating to bulk transfers between schemes arising, for example, as a result of acquisitions and mergers of companies.

Public sector

4.6   Table 4.2 gives an analysis of the data for schemes in the public sector, showing separate figures for the schemes for public corporations including the nationalized industries, for central government, and for local authorities with a subdivision between unfunded schemes, where no specific assets are held against future liabilities, and funded schemes. Practically all of the central government schemes are unfunded. The figures shown are based on data collected by the Department of Trade and Industry, but supplemented by additional details from the Government Actuary's Department's analysis of public sector scheme accounts. For unfunded central and local government schemes the investment income is shown as nil and the employer's contribution

15

is taken as the balance of expenditure not met by employees' contributions or transfer payments. This approach has been followed even for schemes, such as those for teachers and NHS employees, where notional accounts are maintained on the basis of which specific employer contributions are determined, because any excess of income over expenditure is not invested in identifiable assets but forms part of the current receipts of central government.

Table 4.2 Estimates of income and expenditure of public sector pension schemes 1987

£ million

	Public corpor- ations	Central govern- ment	Local authorities		Total public sector
			(f)	(u)	
Income:					
Employers' contributions	1,390	3,990	850	1,380	7,610
Members' contributions	530	650	590	760	2,530
Transfer payments from other schemes	200	90	160	60	510
Rents, dividends and interest	2,030	—	1,420	—	3,450
Miscellaneous income	100	—	30	—	130
Total income	4,250	4,730	3,050	2,200	14,230
Expenditure:					
Pensions to former employees	1,370	3,200	1,080	1,530	7,180
Pensions to dependants of former employees	290	350	100	90	830
Lump sums on death	70	60	30	20	180
Lump sums on retirement	470	850	250	390	1,960
Transfer payments to other pension schemes or arrangements	170	190	180	130	670
Refunds of contributions to members	20	40	30	20	110
Miscellaneous expenditure	130	40	20	20	210
Total expenditure	2,520	4,730	1,690	2,200	11,140
Excess of income over expenditure	1,730	—	1,360	—	3,090
					millions
Numbers of active members	*0.9*	*2.0*	*1.1*	*0.8*	*4.8*
Numbers of pensioners	*0.9*	*1.25*	*0.55*	*0.4*	*3.1*

(f) and (u) relate to funded and unfunded local authority arrangements respectively.

16

Insured schemes

4.7   The data from the present survey do not enable detailed estimates of income and expenditure to be made separately for schemes operated through insurance companies and for self-administered schemes. Particular problems were encountered with the information for schemes which, though in principle self-administered, provided some of their benefits through insurance contracts, eg through the investment of a part of the assets in a managed fund operated by an insurance company. However, on the basis of the provision for the liabilities (the so called 'mathematical reserves') in respect of group scheme business shown in Schedule 4 of insurance companies' statutory returns to the Department of Trade and Industry, an estimate was made of the assets held by insurance companies in respect of this class of business at the end of 1987, at of the order of £40 billion at market values. This relates wholly to private sector schemes as hardly any contributions to public sector schemes are now invested through insurance companies.

Funds invested other than through insurance companies

4.8   In the questionnaire schemes were asked to give the market value of their funds, other than the funds relating to benefits being provided through insurance companies and held by the insurance companies. Estimates of the total funds and the distribution by size at the end of 1987, based on this data, are shown in Table 4.3, which shows that the estimated total market value of assets of private sector pension funds invested other than through insurance companies was £156 billion at the end of 1987. The corresponding figure for public sector funds was £67 billion. Adding the broad estimate of £40 billion for insured schemes gives total assets relating to pension schemes in the region of £260 billion. These totals imply assets averaging around £20,000 per active member or pensioner for private sector schemes. An indication of the rate of growth of the funds, before allowing for changes in the market value of the assets held, is given by the excess of income over expenditure under schemes in the year 1987, which, as shown in Table 4.1, totalled about £14 billion, comprising about £11 billion in the private sector and about £3 billion in the public sector.

Table 4.3 Private sector funds invested other than through insurance contracts

Size of fund (market value)	Number of schemes	Number of members	Market value of funds
£ million		thousands	£ billion
Over 1,000	20	900	54
500–1,000	35	700	24
250–500	65	500	22
100–250	160	800	24
50–100	200	400	11
10–50	700	500	13
Under 10	*	*	8
Total			156

*The small number of schemes with funds of under £10 million yielded by the sampling method and the relatively low response rate to the questionnaires sent to such schemes do not allow an accurate estimate of their number.

Comparisons with national accounts aggregates

4.9   The large sums involved in the operation of pension schemes may usefully be set against aggregates for the national economy of the United Kingdom. The amounts shown in Table 4.1 may be compared with the components of total household income in 1987 (before tax and national insurance contributions) as shown in Table 4.9 of the *United Kingdom National Accounts: 1990 Edition* (the "Blue Book"), as follows:

	£ billion
Total wages, salaries and income in kind	200
Income from self-employment	34
Rents, dividends and interest (gross)	22
Pensions and other benefits from life assurance and superannuation schemes	28
Social security benefits	42
Other current transfers	11
Total household income	337

4.10   The funds of occupational pension schemes can be compared with an estimate of *marketable* personal wealth (i.e. excluding the values of occupational and state pensions) of £1,124 billion in 1987, given in *Inland Revenue Statistics 1990*. They may also be compared with the total financial assets of the personal sector as shown in the Central Statistical Office's *Financial Statistics*. These assets have been provisionally estimated to amount to £842 billion at the end of 1987. Financial assets exclude non-financial assets such as direct investment in property.

5 Types of Schemes and Eligibility for Membership

5.1 This chapter marks the transition to the second part of this report, in which the 10.6 million active members of occupational pension schemes (ie those qualifying for benefits in respect of current service) are shown as classified according to the provisions of the rules of their schemes relating to contributions (Chapter 6), benefits (Chapters 7 to 11), and appointment of trustees (Chapter 12). The present chapter is intended to give an overall view of the main types of scheme encountered and of the eligibility conditions for membership.

5.2 It must be emphasized, however, at this stage that there is no single, precise definition of exactly what pension arrangements constitute a scheme. For instance, similar but separate arrangements made by an employer for several employees with the same insurance company might be regarded for some purposes as separate schemes and for others as a single scheme, whilst the employees might not regard it as a pension *scheme* at all. In principle the approach employed in this survey is to follow the employee's own conception as to whether his pension arrangements constitute a scheme run by his employer or not, as reflected in the replies to the GHS interviewer.

5.3 Another complication is that some employers operate more than one scheme; others share in centralized schemes. The total number of schemes in existence is difficult to determine with any precision, but from this survey it is clear that the number is more than, and possibly considerably more than, 80,000 distinct schemes. Leaving aside the small schemes with twelve or fewer members (the number of which it is difficult to assess partly because of the point mentioned in the preceding paragraph, and partly because of the relatively few such schemes included in the sample), it is clear that although the total number of *members* has fallen a little since the 1983 survey, the number of *schemes* has increased substantially.

Size of membership and numbers of private sector schemes

5.4   In the private sector schemes vary widely in scope – from what are practically individual arrangements to schemes which cover over 100,000 employees of a large company or group. A breakdown of schemes by numbers of members and whether contracted-out is shown in Table 5.1. Two-thirds of the members in the private sector are in some 800 large schemes with over a thousand members, but about one million employees are in small schemes with fewer than a hundred members. The table also shows that it is the larger schemes which tend to be contracted-out.

Table 5.1   Numbers of schemes and of members by sector and size of membership and whether contracted-out

	Contracted-out		Not contracted-out		Total	
Sector	Schemes	Members	Schemes	Members	Schemes	Members
Private sector, by number of members in scheme:		thousands		thousands		thousands
1–12	*	50	*	230	*	280
13–99	10,400	390	8,500	280	18,900	670
100–999	2,900	780	900	230	3,800	1,010
1,000–4,999	520	1,040	110	210	630	1,250
5,000–9,999	70	490	10	80	80	570
10,000 and over	70	1,750	10	270	80	2,020
Totals		4,500		1,300		5,800
Public sector	180	4,800	–	–	180	4,800
Total members (thousands)		9,300		1,300		10,600

*The small number of schemes with 12 or fewer members yielded by the sampling method and the relatively low response rate to the questionnaires sent to such schemes do not allow an accurate estimate of their number, but it appears likely that in total there are between 50,000 and 100,000 of them.

Contracted-out schemes

5.5   As shown in Table 5.1, nearly 80 per cent of scheme members in the private sector and virtually all scheme members in the public sector were in schemes which were contracted-out. When a scheme is contracted-out the members forego the main additional earnings-related pensions benefits under the state scheme and, in return, the national insurance contributions otherwise payable are reduced for both the employee and the employer. At the time of the survey all contracted-out schemes were required to provide for a pension at normal retirement age of at least 1/80th of final salary for each year of service and for a guaranteed minimum pension, corresponding broadly to the earnings-related additional pension foregone in the state scheme. In fact, most schemes in the private sector provided a pension fraction of sixtieths, rather than the minimum of eightieths required for contracting-out, but with provision for part of the benefit to be commuted for a lump sum on retirement. In the public sector the pension benefit is usually eightieths, but there is a lump sum in addition which makes the value of the whole benefit similar to that of a sixtieths pension. The most common arrangements, which are applicable to most of those who are contracted-out in both the public and private sectors alike, are for a personal pension (including lump sum equivalent) based on, or equivalent to, sixtieths of final salary, a widow's pension of one-third or one-half of this, together with a lump sum on death in service, usually of one to three years' salary. Although benefit formulae tend to give pensions that are, for the same nominal final salary, a little higher in the private sector than in the public sector, private sector pensions are not generally fully protected against inflation and are frequently based on pensionable salaries which exclude variable elements such as commission and bonus payments, which may form an important part of private sector remuneration.

Schemes not contracted-out

5.6   About 1.3 million employees, very nearly all in the private sector, are in schemes which are not contracted-out, and thus unless an adjustment is made (see paragraph 7.11) any pension benefits provided are in addition to the full state scheme benefits. These schemes range from those giving a small lump sum gratuity on retirement to those providing, usually for senior executives, benefits up to the Inland Revenue maxima for approved schemes. About 40,000 members are in schemes giving a lump sum but no pension on retirement, and a further 350,000 in schemes providing either a flat-rate pension independent of salary or a pension or lump sum based on the money purchase value of the contributions. About half of the members not contracted-out are in final-salary schemes with a pension fraction of at least eightieths, ie which met the main requirement for contracting-out at the time of the survey.

Schemes by status of employees covered

5.7   This survey, in common with earlier surveys, indicates that many firms of all sizes give larger pension benefits to senior executives than to the rest of their staff employees. Many small companies provide pensions for their managers only. Both of these groups of schemes were described as 'senior executives or management' schemes by scheme managers when answering the survey questionnaire.

5.8   It is still common for employers to have separate schemes for their works employees, with a lower scale of benefits. Such employees are variously described as hourly-paid, weekly-paid, operatives, manual workers, industrials, or just 'other than staff employees'. An important factor is that state pension benefits are larger for the lower-paid in proportion to pre-retirement earnings than for higher-paid workers.

5.9   The numbers of members of the various categories of schemes according to the status of employees to which they are open is shown in Table 5.2. For the reason given in paragraph 5.7 above, the category *senior staff only* in this table is a mixture of small schemes operated by large companies with more than one scheme and of the schemes of small companies which just cover a few of their employees.

5.10   The trend detected in 1983 towards greater segregation by status in schemes appears to have been reversed by 1987. In the private sector there has been a reduction in the number of members in all categories of segregated schemes.

Table 5.2 Membership of schemes that cover employees of a particular status

thousands

Status covered	Private sector	Public sector	Total
Senior staff only	120	—	120
Staff employees*	1,170	700	1,870
Staff and works employees	440	—	440
Works employees	510	200	710
Senior staff, staff and works employees	3,240	3,700	6,940
Closed schemes	320	200	520
Totals	5,800	4,800	10,600

*Includes schemes open to staff and senior staff employees.

5.11   In the public sector there are separate arrangements for manual employees in some of the major nationalized industries. In the local government scheme and in the scheme applying to the majority of National Health Service workers there is no difference in benefits, but the contribution rate for manual employees is one per cent less than for staff; however, these schemes are each regarded as one single scheme in this survey, despite the fact that in the case of the local government scheme there is a large number of separately invested funds.

Eligibility for membership

5.12   Few employers include all their employees in pension schemes as a matter of course; frequently temporary employees are excluded, or those working only part-time. Many companies only cover certain categories of staff. In some employments membership was voluntary in 1987. (Because of a change in the law, this now applies generally.) Some employers require employees to attain a specific age or to work a minimum period of service before they are admitted to membership. The reasons for non-membership are dealt with in detail in the remainder of this chapter.

Exclusions from membership

5.13   On the basis of the replies of employees in the GHS sample it would appear that in 1987 about one million employees were excluded from their employer's pension scheme because they were too young or had service which was too short and about three million were excluded for other reasons, for instance because the scheme did not cover part-time or manual employees. Nearly seven million employees were employed by firms which the employees said had no pension scheme (though possibly there was a scheme for some employees of which the respondent was not aware). As might be expected there is a tendency for the proportion of employees with no employer's scheme to decrease with increasing size of the establishment in which the employee works. More details of the numbers excluded from membership are shown analysed by sector in Table 5.3 and according to whether the employment is full-time or part-time in Table 5.4. These numbers are derived from the percentage figures obtained in the 1987 GHS. Chapter 7 of the report *General Household Survey 1987* also gives percentage coverage figures for full-time employees by industry, size of establishment, age and salary.

5.14   The main reasons for exclusion from membership differ for full-time employees and part-time employees. About a quarter of full-time employees worked for employers with no scheme, leaving about 15 per cent of both male and female full-time employees not in their employer's scheme when the employer has one for some employees. Of these about 40 per cent were ineligible because they were too young or had insufficient service. Over 4 million part-time employees were not members of pension schemes, of which just under one half were excluded from membership for reasons other than age or service and most of the remainder worked for employers who did not have a pension scheme. As already mentioned the analysis of the reasons for non-membership of a scheme is based on replies from employees and not from employers. The split between the situation where the employer has no scheme and where he has a scheme but it does not include particular grades of employees may not be wholly reliable as the employees questioned may not always have been aware of the wider situation in their firms.

do with table on p t ezr — ✗

Table 5.3 Numbers of employees not in pension schemes by cause of exclusion and according to sector

millions

Reason for exclusion	Private sector		Public sector		
	Men	Women	Men	Women	Total
Employer has no scheme	3.1	3.5	0.1*	0.2*	6.9
Employer has a scheme, but the employee:					
is too young or has service too short	0.5	0.4	—	—	0.9
has opted not to join, or is ineligible					
because part-time or for other reasons	0.9	1.0	0.2	1.1	3.2
Total numbers not in pension schemes	4.5	4.9	0.3	1.3	11.0
Total numbers who are in schemes	4.4	1.4	2.8	2.0	10.6
Total numbers of employees	8.9	6.3	3.1	3.3	21.6

*Unlikely to be correct as virtually all public sector employers have schemes.

Table 5.4 Numbers of employees not in pension schemes by cause of exclusion and according to whether in full-time or part-time employment

millions

Reason for exclusion	Full-time		Part-time		
	Men	Women	Men	Women	Total
Employer has no scheme	2.9	1.5	0.3	2.2	6.9
Employer has a scheme, but the employee:					
is too young or has service too short	0.6	0.3	—	—	0.9
has opted not to join, or is ineligible					
because part-time or for other reasons	0.9	0.5	0.1	1.7	3.2
Total numbers not in pension schemes	4.4	2.3	0.4	3.9	11.0
Total numbers who are in schemes	7.1	3.0	0.1	0.4	10.6
Total numbers of employees	11.5	5.3	0.5	4.3	21.6

6   Contributions to Schemes

6.1   As indicated in Chapter 4, a large part of the income of pension schemes consists of the contributions from employers and from members. Taking all schemes together these are roughly in the ratio of three to one. However, individual schemes can vary from those where no contributions are required from the members (except possibly for some optional benefits) to a few schemes where the only contribution income being received by the scheme is from the members, because, for example, the employer was taking a contribution holiday as contributions paid in earlier years had proved to be too high. The numbers of members in private sector schemes paying various proportions of total contributions are shown in Table 6.1.

Table 6.1   Numbers of members paying various proportions of the total contributions: private sector

Proportion paid by members	Number of members
	thousands
n/a*	80
nil	900
1–9%†	200
10–19%	250
20–29%	940
30–39%	1,370
40–49%	770
50–99%	940
100%	350
Totals	5,800

*not applicable because neither employer nor members were contributing in 1987
†includes schemes in which members contribute for widows' benefits only or make voluntary contributions only

Members' contributions

6.2   In the tables below, *percentage of salary* indicates that the contributions are assessed as a uniform percentage which is applied to the salary as defined for scheme purposes, which may exclude certain elements of remuneration. Thus, an amount might be disregarded to allow for national insurance benefits, or bonuses and overtime payments might be omitted. A type of contribution occasionally found in schemes covering only manual employees is the flat contribution which does not vary with earnings or age, but may in some cases vary according to job status.

6.3   Some schemes, notably the Civil Service scheme, but also a few schemes in the private sector, require direct contributions only for widows' benefits. In the remainder of this chapter these schemes are nevertheless classed as contributory even though the contributions required for widows' benefits are relatively small. (This represents a change from the treatment in previous surveys.) Table 6.2 gives details of the form of members' contributions in 1987. Contributions other than those based on a percentage of salary have become very rare.

Table 6.2   Numbers of members according to method of calculation of their contributions and their contracting-out status

thousands

Contributions	Private sector		Public sector	Total
	Contracted-out	Not contracted-out	Contracted-out	
Percentage of salary	3,820	800	4,480	9,100
Other	—	80	—	80
All contributory schemes	3,820	880	4,480	9,180
Non-contributory schemes	680	420	320	1,420
Totals	4,500	1,300	4,800	10,600

Levels of members' contribution

6.4   Table 6.3 shows that in the private sector a contribution rate of 5 per cent of salary has for many years been the most common rate of contribution. In the public sector the most common level is 6 per cent. Where the contribution rate varies within the same scheme, for example by sex or class, the higher or highest rate has been taken. For the 4.6 million members contributing a percentage of salary to the private sector schemes in 1987 the average contribution was about £520. More details are given in Tables 6.3 and 6.4.

Table 6.3   Numbers of private sector members paying contributions of various percentages of salary

millions

Percentage of salary	1975	1979	1983	1987
Under 2%	0.1	0.2	0.1	0.1
2% and under 3%	0.6	0.3	0.3	0.3
3% and under 4%	0.5	0.4	0.6	0.4
4% and under 5%	0.5	0.6	0.5	0.6
5% and under 6%	1.6	2.2	1.8	1.8
6% and under 7%	0.7	0.8	1.1	1.2
7% and over	0.1	0.1	0.2	0.2
Total paying percentages	4.1	4.6	4.6	4.6
Non-contributory or other basis	1.8	1.5	1.2	1.2
Totals	5.9	6.1	5.8	5.8

Table 6.4   Numbers of members paying contributions of various percentages of salary

thousands

Percentage of salary	Private sector		Public sector	Total
	Contracted-out	Not contracted-out	Contracted-out	
Under 2%	40	30	680	750
2% and under 3%	190	110	—	300
3% and under 4%	310	160	—	470
4% and under 5%	500	100	50	650
5% and under 6%	1,580	190	150	1,920
6% and under 7%*	1,100	80	3,250	4,430
7% and over	100	130	350	580
Total paying percentages	3,820	800	4,480	9,100
Non-contributory or other basis	680	500	320	1,500
Totals	4,500	1,300	4,800	10,600

*Includes some groups of employees only paying 5%: see paragraph 6.4

6.5   In the 1987 survey information was sought from private sector employers as to whether contributions are based on a reduced salary in order to take account of state scheme benefits and contributions. The results are shown in Table 6.5. In the public sector virtually all contributions are based on unreduced salaries.

Table 6.5 Numbers of private sector members by whether contributions are based on reduced salary

thousands

Contributions basis	Contracted-out	Not contracted-out	Total
Salary reduced	1,700	150	1,850
Salary not reduced	2,120	650	2,770
Not applicable	680	500	1,180
Totals	4,500	1,300	5,800

7   Benefits on Normal Retirement

7.1   As in previous surveys, the term 'pension scheme' has been interpreted broadly. Returns were also requested from schemes which provided only lump sums on retirement and such schemes have been treated as pension schemes in this report. Schemes providing only lump sums on death have been ignored, except where they operate together with a retirement benefits scheme.

7.2   The majority of private sector scheme members are in schemes providing only a pension benefit at retirement but with an option of exchanging part of their pension benefits for a lump sum payment at retirement. A few private sector schemes provide for a lump sum in all cases in addition to the pension, but this form of benefit is the norm in the public sector where a benefit wholly expressed in the form of a pension with a commutation option is only found in a few schemes, such as the scheme for the police. About 40,000 people are members of schemes providing only a lump sum benefit at retirement.

Pension age

7.3   The 'normal retirement age', as defined by the Inland Revenue, is the age specified in the rules of a pension scheme at which the members normally retire and receive their pension. It should be borne in mind that members may well retire earlier or later than this 'normal' age with the agreement of their employer.

7.4   Table 7.1 shows that the normal retirement ages in occupational pension schemes in the private sector still tend to coincide with those of the state scheme. In 1987, 75 per cent of male members were in schemes with a pension age of 65 and 85 per cent of female members were in schemes with a pension age of 60, but there is a clear trend towards equalization. The proportion of men entitled to retire earlier than 65 had risen from about 15 to about 25 per cent since the previous survey, while the proportion of women with a retirement age above 60 had risen from 5 per cent or less to between 10 and 15 per cent.

Though none are shown because none appeared in the GHS sample on which this survey is based, there are a few special groups in the private sector which have a normal retirement age for men of under 60 years.

Table 7.1 Numbers of members of schemes according to normal retirement age

thousands

Normal retirement age	Private sector		Public sector		Both sectors	
	1983	1987	1983	1987	1983	1987
Men						
Under 60	—	—	530	500	530	500
60	260	800	1,320	1,200	1,580	2,000
Between 60 and 65	350	230	850	700	1,200	930
65	3,770	3,370	710	400	4,480	3,770
Totals	4,380	4,400	3,410	2,800	7,790	7,200
Women						
Under 60	90	10	330	400	420	410
60	1,260	1,210	1,110	1,040	2,370	2,250
Between 60 and 65	30	40	450	550	480	590
65	30	140	10	10	40	150
Totals	1,410	1,400	1,900	2,000	3,310	3,400
Combined totals	5,790	5,800	5,310	4,800	11,100	10,600

7.5   There is a somewhat different pattern in the public sector, where 43 per cent of male employees have a normal retirement age of 60 and a further 18 per cent have a normal retirement age of under 60. The majority of those tabulated as having a normal retirement age of between 60 and 65 are local government scheme members, who may retire between those ages provided they have completed 25 years of service. Those with a pension age of less than 60 (of either sex) are in arduous employment, involving significant mental strain or requiring a high standard of physical fitness, for example the uniformed services.

Pension formula

7.6 Private sector pensions are for over 90 per cent of members calculated on a 'final salary' basis, ie based on salary at retirement or averaged over the final years or months of service. The usual approach is to calculate the pension as a fraction of final salary multiplied by the length of the member's service.

7.7 *Average earnings* (or *average salary*) schemes calculate the pension as a fraction of the total salary earned throughout service. Both these and pensions awarded as a flat sum per year of service have suffered a sharp decline in popularity because of the effects of inflation, and have now virtually disappeared. Consequently, the *other basis* arrangements shown in Table 7.2 are mainly 'money purchase', where the pension is calculated as the amount purchased by the contributions made by the member and employer from time to time. There are also a few schemes in which the career salary is revalued to take inflation into account. There continues to be a small number of members in lump sum only schemes.

7.8 Table 7.2 gives further details for the private sector from the current survey, according to whether or not the scheme was contracted-out. Public sector schemes are almost all based on final salary and contracted-out.

Table 7.2 Numbers of private sector members according to pension formula and whether or not contracted-out of the state additional pension

thousands

Pension formula	Contracted-out	Not contracted-out	Total
Final salary	4,500	780	5,280
Other basis	—	480	480
No pension	—	40	40
Totals	4,500	1,300	5,800

Adaptation to national insurance

7.9 Many schemes have a pension benefit formula incorporating an adjustment to allow for the fact that retired members will also receive a pension from the state scheme. The adjustment may be in respect of the state flat-rate basic pension or the earnings-related additional pension where a scheme is not contracted-out, or, in some cases, both.

7.10   The most common approach among schemes making some adjustment is to use a reduced salary as a basis for members' contributions (if any) and pensions. The deduction, which may be different for the contributions and the benefits calculations, is often related to either the basic state pension for a single person or the lower earnings limit for national insurance contributions—which under current legislation are in principle the same and are treated as such for the purposes of Table 7.3.

7.11   Among schemes which are not contracted-out an adjustment is sometimes made to the pension to allow for the state additional pension, usually in addition to an adjustment for the flat-rate pension. A deduction which accurately reflects the relevant state scheme benefit can be relatively complicated; a somewhat simpler approach provides a lower pension fraction in respect of that part of final salary which falls below the upper earnings limit under the state scheme.

Table 7.3 Numbers of private sector members according to adjustment to the pension for national insurance

thousands

Adjustment	Contracted-out	Not contracted-out	Total
None	2,200	850	3,050
Pension calculated on reduced salary	1,700	200	1,900
Calculated pension otherwise reduced	600	100	700
Accrual fraction varies	—	150	150
Totals	4,500	1,300	5,800

7.12   In the public sector some schemes have a reduction in pensionable salary to take some account of national insurance benefits, but it is usually a fairly small one.

Other adjustments to pensionable salary

7.13   Many final-salary schemes use a definition of salary for pension purposes which excludes fluctuating payments such as commission, bonuses and overtime, and thus may be at a lower level than the actual income of the employee. Where fluctuating payments are not excluded they often receive special treatment, for example they may be averaged over a period of years or months in order to provide a more stable figure for contribution and benefit

34

purposes. Table 7.4 gives an indication of the extent to which pensionable salary excludes fluctuating income. The *not applicable* line includes schemes in which the benefits are not related to salary and schemes of employers who do not generally have any arrangements for making overtime and similar fluctuating payments (for instance the Armed Forces and teachers). The table covers the general position under a scheme, but sometimes special arrangements exist for those employees within a company who depend heavily on commission or bonuses for their income.

Table 7.4 Number of members according to treatment of fluctuating payments when calculating pensionable salary

thousands

| Fluctuating payments | Private sector | | Public sector | Total |
	Contracted-out	Not contracted-out		
All payments included	940	280	420	1,640
All fluctuating payments excluded	1,880	590	3,180	5,650
Some included, some excluded	1,550	270	100	1,920
Not applicable	130	160	1,100	1,390
Totals	4,500	1,300	4,800	10,600

Final salary

7.14 The method of calculation of 'final' salary from a member's 'pensionable' salary in the period prior to retirement (which may already include adjustments as described in the preceding paragraphs) can vary considerably from scheme to scheme. In periods of high inflation these variations can result in significant differences in the levels of pension provided by otherwise identical schemes. 'Final' salary may be equal to the actual annual rate of salary at retirement, or it can be the average annual salary received over a period prior to retirement, commonly one or three years. Where a longer averaging period is used, the level of benefit will be more sensitive to the rate of inflation. As Table 7.5 shows, a period of one year (or less) is the norm in the public sector and also applies to 55 per cent of the members in the private sector—as compared with only 45 per cent in 1983. Generally the averaging period is the period immediately prior to retirement, but for a number of schemes in the private sector it is the period up to the 'scheme anniversary', which may be up to twelve months before retirement.

Table 7.5 Numbers of members in final-salary schemes according to numbers of years earnings averaged to obtain 'final' salary

thousands

Number of years	Private sector	Public sector	Total
1 or less	2,930	4,620	7,550
2 years	230	—	230
3 years	2,060	180	2,240
5 years	60	—	60
Totals	5,280	4,800	10,080

7.15   For some employees, particularly many manual workers, earnings in the last few years before retirement can be lower than at some earlier period, and for this reason many schemes in both the public and private sectors provide that an earlier averaging period may be used for calculating 'final' salary if this would produce a higher result. For example, a common provision is that the pension can be based on the best three years in the ten-year period before retirement. The effect of inflation in recent years has reduced the value of this sort of provision, although a few schemes overcome the problem by adjusting all salary figures used in the calculation in accordance with some index of inflation to the date of retirement. Table 7.6 gives an indication of the total period prior to retirement which may be taken into account in the final-salary calculation, ie over which the best average salary figure is taken. A number of schemes have periods different from those shown in the table and these cases have been amalgamated with the next higher period shown. *No comparison* indicates that only the latest averaging period can be used for calculating final salary. As stated above, in some private sector schemes final salary is calculated on the better of two completely different bases, for example either salary in the year prior to retirement or, if higher, average salary in the best three years out of ten years prior to retirement. About 600,000 people are members of schemes offering a 'better of two bases' final-salary definition of this type and in the table the numbers involved have been entered in the category involving the shorter averaging period amongst the bases offered by the scheme.

Table 7.6 Numbers of members in final-salary schemes according to number of years' earnings averaged to obtain 'final' salary and the number of years over which the best average salary figure is taken

thousands

Sector and averaging period	Number of years over which best average salary is taken				
	No comparison	3 years	5 years	10 or more years	Total
Private sector:					
1 year or less	2,040	420	370	100	2,930
2 years	170	—	—	60	230
3 years	1,000	—	30	1,030	2,060
5 years	50	—	—	10	60
Totals	3,260	420	400	1,200	5,280
Public sector:					
1 year or less	1,925	2,690	5	—	4,620
2 years	—	—	—	—	—
3 years	65	—	—	115	180
Totals	1,990	2,690	5	115	4,800
Both sectors	5,250	3,110	405	1,315	10,080

7.16   In response to the survey question about revaluation of earnings in the averaging period in order to mitigate the effects of inflation, it would appear that about 300,000 people are members of private sector schemes which contain such a provision.

Pension fraction

7.17   Table 7.7 shows the levels of benefit provided in final salary schemes. For this purpose any lump sum payable on retirement, other than by way of commutation of pension benefit, has been treated as a pension of the equivalent amount and added to the pension. The total 'equivalent pension fraction' has then been analysed.

37

Table 7.7 Numbers of members with various fractions (including lump sum equivalents) in final-salary schemes

thousands

Equivalent pension fraction	Private sector		Public sector	Total
	Contracted-out	Not contracted-out		
Better than 60ths (if service less than 40 years)	470	60	650	1,180
60ths	2,990	370	4,000	7,360
Between 60ths and 80ths	350	70	130	550
80ths	690	170	20	880
Less than 80ths	—	110	—	110
Totals	4,500	780	4,800	10,080

7.18   The prevalence of schemes giving an equivalent pension fraction per year of service of sixtieths or better can be seen from Table 7.7, both among those contracted-out and those not contracted-out. There appears, however, to have been a small increase in the number of those contracted-out on the basis of schemes granting only eighteenths. There is a tendency for schemes for staff and executive employees to provide pension fractions of sixtieths or better, whereas most of the schemes providing a fraction of eightieths appear to cover mainly manual workers. Even within the same company, it is not uncommon for a higher fraction to be provided for staff than for works employees. An important factor here is that for lower-paid workers state benefits are larger in proportion to pre-retirement earnings than they are for the higher paid. Some schemes for senior executives provide a pension of a fixed fraction of salary (perhaps one-half or two-thirds, subject to a minimum period of service of 10 to 20 years).

8   Early and Late Retirement

Ill-health pensions

8.1   In nearly all schemes there is provision to pay a pension commencing immediately on premature retirement on grounds of ill-health; in fact, many schemes in the private sector (covering 32 per cent of members as compared with 20 per cent in 1983) are now providing ill-health pensions of the same amount as would have been paid at the normal retirement age, ie based on full potential service and without reduction for early payment. On the other hand, about 30 per cent of members of private sector schemes would, on retiring on ill-health, receive a pension calculated on the basis of their accrued service only, ie the actual service rendered before ill-health retirement, thus taking no account of service which would subsequently have earned pension had ill-health not intervened. In almost 60 per cent of these cases (ie 17 per cent of total membership) the pension would be further reduced because it was being paid from an earlier age than for normal retirement; this reduction can be as much as one-half.

8.2   Virtually all public sector schemes and many other private sector schemes (covering a further 15 per cent of members) provide ill-health pensions which have a basis somewhere between these extremes of full potential service and of service up to the date of ill-health retirement only. The service to count is sometimes then described as 'enhanced' (see glossary in Appendix A3).

8.3   In general, as Table 8.1 shows, there has been some improvement between 1983 and 1987 in the provision of ill-health retirement benefits. In particular, there has been a significant rise in the number of people for whom a separate Permanent Health Insurance scheme is in force and a fall in the number only receiving the accrued pension.

Table 8.1 Numbers of private sector members according to ill-health provision

millions

Basis of pension	1983	1987
Better than accrued pension	2.6	2.7
Accrued pension only	1.25	0.75
Less than accrued pension	1.65	1.55
Separate Permanent Health Insurance	0.3	0.8
Totals	5.8	5.8

8.4   More complete details of ill-health provision found in the current survey for the two sectors are shown in Table 8.2. *Other basis* schemes include some money purchase arrangements, some schemes in which the pension is based on a percentage (independent of service) of salary at or near ill-health retirement and some schemes which provide a disability lump sum in addition to a scheme pension. A significant and increasing number of members are covered by separate Permanent Health Insurance schemes. Such schemes normally provide a pension up to normal retirement age only, to be replaced by a pension from the pension fund itself, which may be at a different rate, possibly based on the service that could have been earned to normal retirement if ill-health had not intervened.

Table 8.2 Numbers of members according to ill-health provision

thousands

Basis of pension	Private sector	Public sector	Total
Full potential service	1,850	200	2,050
Service to date enhanced	840	4,440	5,280
Service to date only:			
unreduced	750	160	910
reduced	1,020	—	1,020
Separate Permanent Health Insurance	800	—	800
Other basis	200	—	200
No pension or discretionary	340	—	340
Totals	5,800	4,800	10,600

8.5 From the questionnaire responses it would appear that about 170,000 people are members of private sector schemes where the provision of ill-health pension benefits is discretionary. Rule books were not examined in 1987, but a number of those examined in 1983 specifically provided for the payment of higher rates of ill-health pension at the employer's (or trustees') discretion. Some schemes provide benefits which vary with the degree of incapacity, for example a higher level of benefit on very serious disability, or a lower level of benefit if they do not qualify for the 'usual' ill-health benefit because their illness is not sufficiently severe to incapacitate them. Special arrangements may also be made for those injured at work or who contract an industrial disease.

Other early retirement

8.6 Most private sector schemes have provision for retirement on immediate pension for any member over a certain age (for instance, 50), or within a certain period of the member's normal retirement date, such as five years. Such early retirement may require the consent of the employer. Some schemes have special provisions for early pensions on redundancy. The majority of schemes require a minimum period of service to be completed after admission to the scheme before an early retirement pension is available, and this minimum is not necessarily the same as that applying to a pension at normal retirement age described in Chapter 5. In many schemes early retirement can take place on the initiative of either the member or the employer, though this is not always the case as Table 8.3 shows. The question of whose initiative it is can affect the circumstances in which pensions may be granted on early retirement, for example the age of the person concerned. This is illustrated in Table 8.4.

Table 8.3 Numbers of private sector members according to on whose initiative early retirement (other than on ill-health) can take place

thousands

Early pension	Number
No pension available	290
On initiative of member only	680
On initiative of employer only	1,230
On initiative of either	3,600
Total	5,800

41

Table 8.4 Proportion of private sector members with provision for early retirement (other than on ill-health) at minimum age shown

percentages

Minimum age	Initiative of employer	Initiative of member
	%	%
50	80	67
Between 50 and 60	18	25
60 or over	2	8

8.7   The majority of schemes, if they have any special provisions regarding the amount of pension to be paid to an employee retiring early (other than on ill-health) at the employer's request or with his approval, base the early retirement pension on accrued service to the date of early retirement and then apply a reduction factor. Usually, the accrued pension without any reduction would be available to the retiring employee as a preserved pension commencing at normal retirement date – the reduction allows for the pension to commence at an earlier age instead. The amount of the reduction, however, can be more favourable than would result from strict application of compound interest and life expectancy factors.

8.8   Some schemes provide an early retirement pension calculated by applying a reduction factor to the pension based on full potential service to normal retirement date. Other schemes provide on early retirement an immediate pension based on accrued service and without reduction, but the conditions under which such pensions are available tend to be very restricted, for example the pensions may be limited to members over age 60 or within five years of normal retirement date and possibly require a long minimum period of service. Public sector schemes commonly have no provision for early retirement apart from the normal early leaver's benefits, and any special arrangements for employees who are declared redundant are made outside the pension scheme.

8.9   As described in Chapter 7, many schemes provide a pension at normal retirement date which is based on a formula incorporating a deduction to allow for the pension that will be provided by the state scheme. Many of these schemes do not apply this deduction when calculating the pension available on early retirement, but only reduce it when the state pension commences. An even incidence of total pension income during retirement is thus provided. In a few schemes a member retiring early is given an option to exchange the usual level pension for a pension at a higher rate until state pension age and a lower rate thereafter.

Deferment of retirement

8.10   The normal practice in both the public and private sectors is for payment of pension to be withheld if a member continues in service after normal retiring age and for an increased pension to be put into payment on eventual retirement. In the public sector no distinction is commonly made between service before and after the normal retiring age, both periods ranking for the retirement benefits in the usual way, but with a maximum of 40 to 45 years which may count. The pension and lump sum are based on the salary averaged over the appropriate period prior to actual retirement: contributions by the member and, where appropriate, by the employer continue until retirement. A rather different system is usual in the private sector, and is also found in nationalized industries, in which contributions cease at the normal retirement age and subsequent service does not rank for pension but the pension eventually awarded is increased to allow both for the amount of pension foregone during the further service and for the interest earned on the reserves backing the pension during the deferment period.

9 Post Retirement Pensions Increases

9.1   Employers were asked for the percentage amounts by which pensions in payment were increased in the years 1984, 1985 and 1986, and also what increase was required by the rules of the scheme.

Private sector

9.2   The dates of the most recent increases were examined. Of pensions in payment in 1987, 80 per cent received an increase during 1986, but one-sixth had received no increase at all during the period 1984-86. Where pensions in payment are increased, it would seem now to be rare for this to be done other than on a regular basis. The numbers of pensions according to the date of the most recent increase can be seen in Table 9.1, which also shows that, on average for those pensioners who did receive an increase in their pensions, the amount of that increase broadly matched the increase in the cost of living over the three-year period.

Table 9.1 Proportions of private sector pensions according to date of most recent pensions increase ' and average level of increase

Year	Percentage with last increase in year	Percentage receiving increase in year	Average increase (%)		RPI increase (to mid-year) %
			All pensions	Increased pensions only	
1984	0.8	76.2	3.8	5.0	5.0
1985	2.0	77.2	4.2	5.4	6.1
1986	80.8	80.8	3.4	4.2	3.4
Total	83.6				
Average 1984-1986	—	—	3.8	4.8	4.8

9.3   Table 9.2 gives an analysis of the pensions increases awarded in 1986 according to the rate of increase and shows that the average increase conceals wide variations between schemes. Further reference to the relationship between pensions increases and changes in the cost of living is made in paragraph 9.6 below.

Table 9.2   Numbers of private sector pensions according to pensions increase in 1986

Amount of increase	Number of pensions
	thousands
8% or more	110
6% or more but less than 8%	160
4% or more but less than 6%	980
2% or more but less than 4%	810
2% or less	280
No increase	560
Total	2,900

9.4   Table 9.3 shows that for most of the pensions in payment in contracted-out schemes the increases referred to above and shown in the tables apply only to the pension in excess of the guaranteed minimum pension. (At the time of the survey the state scheme provided the whole of the inflation proofing on the GMP.) For schemes not contracted-out, however, the increases usually apply to the whole of the pension in payment.

Table 9.3   Numbers of private sector members according to the part of the pension in payment that is expected to be subject to increase

thousands

Part of pension	Contracted-out	Not contracted-out	Total
Full pension	880	700	1,580
Pension in excess of GMP only	2,890	—	2,890
Other limitations	250	60	310
No increase	480	540	1,020
Totals	4,500	1,300	5,800

Increases promised in rules

9.5   As can be seen from Table 9.4, almost half of private sector pensions in payment had increases promised by the rules of the scheme. Increases in line with the Retail Prices Index (the RPI) or other formulae linked in some way to the cost of living were provided for in some cases but the guaranteed increases were usually limited to a fixed rate. In about 50 per cent of cases where increases were promised the amount was limited to 3 per cent a year; other specified rates were 2½, 4 and 5 per cent a year and the average limit was about 3½ per cent a year. This represents a continuing improvement on the position in 1979 when only one-fifth of pensions were guaranteed regular increases, of which virtually all were only promised up to 3 per cent a year. Despite the fact that some pensions increases are often guaranteed in the rules of schemes, additional discretionary increases still form a large part of the increases actually granted, and of the 2.34 million pensions shown in Table 9.2 as having been increased during 1986 about 1.47 million were either wholly discretionary or else in excess of the amount guaranteed in the rules.

Table 9.4 Numbers of private sector pensions according to increases promised by rules

Amount of promised increase	Number of pensions
	thousands
5%	300
4%	110
3%	610
2% to 2½%	40
Proportion of cost of living	60
Full cost of living	170
None	1,610
Total	2,900

Pensions increases and the cost of living

9.6   During the period covered by the pensions increases shown in Table 9.1, the annual rate of price inflation was between about 3 per cent and 6 per cent. There was thus a considerable reduction in the rate of inflation compared with the late 1970's and early 1980's when inflation was over 10 per cent a year. Private sector schemes have not generally awarded pensions increases to match price rises when inflation has been high, but it appears that many took the opportunity of lower rates of inflation to grant increases in excess of the inflation rate, thus making up for past shortfalls, though other schemes continued to give no increases or increases below the rate of inflation.

Public sector

9.7   Almost all pensions paid by public sector employers are indexed to the cost of living, most of them in accordance with the Pensions (Increase) Acts and nearly all of the remainder at present follow a similar pattern although not required to do so by their scheme rules. Public service pensions received an increase of 5.1 per cent in November 1984, 7 per cent in November 1985 and 1.1 per cent in July 1986. The increases normally only apply to the part of the pension which is in excess of the GMP.

10   Death Benefits

10.1   The general pattern of benefits on death in service is for a lump sum to be paid with, in most cases, provision for a widow's, widower's or dependant's pension. In addition to these benefits there is sometimes a return of the member's own contributions (if any), particularly where no widow's pension is payable. This return of members' contributions may be with or without compound interest. In a few schemes the level of the lump sum benefit depends on whether or not a member leaves a widow or other dependant who is eligible for a pension.

Lump sum benefits to married men

10.2   In 1987 the proportion of male members of pension schemes where a lump sum (other than a refund of the member's own contributions) was provided for on the death in service of a married man was 94 per cent.

10.3   In the private sector lump sums paid on death in service are usually defined as a multiple of salary. Table 10.1 shows that over 80 per cent of male members would receive a lump sum in this form. In addition there is a small proportion of cases where the multiple is not constant, but varies over broad ranges of age or lengths of service. In the public sector the lump sum usually depends on both salary and length of service, the 'service' for this purpose often being enhanced, though some public sector schemes now provide lump sums of multiples of salary. The distribution by multiple of annual salary where benefit is in this form, in Table 10.2, shows that the level of benefit has continued to improve, with 57 per cent now covered for at least three times annual salary compared with 39 per cent in the 1983 survey. A refund of contributions may be given in addition to other benefits, but this is becoming less common.

Table 10.1 Numbers of male members according to mode of calculation of lump sum benefit on death (if married) in service and whether a refund of contributions is payable in addition

thousands

Mode of calculation of lump sum	Private sector		Public sector		Total
	Without contribution refund	With contribution refund	Without contribution refund	With contribution refund	
Multiple of salary	2,740	810	800	40	4,390
Fraction of (salary times service)	170	50	1,790	—	2,010
Flat amount	30	—	—	—	30
Other method	300	50	—	—	350
No lump sum or only contribution return	200	50	170	—	420
Totals	3,440	960	2,760	40	7,200

Table 10.2 Numbers of private sector male members with a lump sum benefit in the form of a multiple of salary (if married), according to the multiple and whether a refund of contributions is payable in addition

thousands

Lump sum as a multiple of annual salary	Without contribution refund	With contribution refund	Total
Under 1	—	—	—
1 and under 2	110	30	140
2 and under 3	1,130	260	1,390
3 and under 4	800	290	1,090
4	700	230	930
Totals	2,740	810	3,550

10.4 In the public sector practice varies between the main public service schemes for central and local government employees and the schemes of the public corporations. For the former the lump sum is usually between one and one and a half times salary, without a return of contributions, whilst the public corporation schemes now grant a benefit of a multiple of salary, which in some cases has been increased in recent years. In nearly all public sector schemes there is no distinction in the amount of the death benefit according to sex or marital status.

Death benefits for single men and women

10.5   For almost 90 per cent of private sector scheme members, and for more or less all public sector scheme members, the lump sum death benefit payable does not vary according to the marital status of the deceased member. For about 10 per cent of private sector scheme members the benefit is lower for unmarried people, and for about 2 per cent it is higher for unmarried people. The difference in these cases is usually one or two times the annual salary. A common provision is that a refund of contributions is made only if no continuing pension is payable.

Widows' pensions

10.6   During the 1970s there was a dramatic increase in the proportion of male members of private sector schemes whose widows would have an entitlement to a widow's pension should they die in service; to a large extent this increase could have been the result of schemes altering their benefit structure to comply with the contracting-out requirements of the Social Security Pensions Act 1975. In 1971 only 39 per cent had entitlement to a widow's pension and in 1975 the proportion was still only 54 per cent. By 1979, however, the proportion had risen to about 90 per cent and has since remained at that level. For both private and public sector schemes combined the proportion increased from 56 per cent in 1971 to 94 per cent in 1979, and in 1983 and in 1987 the proportion has remained at that level. Details of the mode of calculations of these widows' pensions are given in Table 10.3 for all male members of schemes. The *other methods* group includes schemes which offer to convert a lump sum into a widow's pension or to provide a widow's pension at the member's option (in exchange for a reduced prospective pension or a higher rate of contribution).

Table 10.3 Numbers of male members according to mode of calculation of widow's pension on death in service

thousands

Mode of calculation	Private sector	Public sector	Total
From member's salary and service	3,600	2,800	6,400
From member's salary only	180	—	180
Other methods	170	—	170
No widow's pension	450	—	450
Totals	4,400	2,800	7,200

10.7   Table 10.4 shows the levels of benefits provided where the pension is calculated from the member's salary and service. The fractions applying in the private sector show continuing improvement, with 77 per cent now covered for 1/120ths or better as compared with 60 per cent in the 1983 survey. In private sector schemes most members—it is estimated two-thirds—have their pension calculated using full potential service. This is true for less than 10 per cent of public sector scheme members, most—about three quarters—of whom have their pension calculated under arrangements whereby the actual service is enhanced, but not normally to the full potential service.

Table 10.4 Numbers of male members in schemes with widow's pension on death in service based on salary and service according to widow's pension fraction

thousands

Fraction per year of service	Private sector	Public sector	Total
100ths or better	480	—	480
Between 100ths and 120ths	150	140	290
120ths	2,130	—	2,130
Between 120ths and 160ths	250	—	250
160ths	500	2,660	3,160
Less than 160ths	90	—	90
Totals	3,600	2,800	6,400

Widowers' pensions

10.8 There has been an increase in the availability of widowers' pensions in private sector schemes. By 1987 about 67 per cent of women in private sector schemes were in schemes which provided for widowers' pensions in all circumstances, and a further 6 per cent in schemes which provided for dependent widowers only. The corresponding percentages for widows' pensions were 85 per cent of men in schemes which provided widows' pensions in all circumstances, and a further 2 per cent in schemes which provided for dependent widows only. Details of provision for widowers' pensions are shown in Table 10.5 below.

Table 10.5 Numbers of female members according to provision of widowers' pensions on death in service

thousands

Provision for widowers' pensions	Private sector	Public sector	Total
All widowers	930	410	1,340
Dependent widowers	90	30	120
None, or option only	380	1,560	1,940
Totals	1,400	2,000	3,400

Death benefits after retirement

10.9 Most occupational pension schemes provide not only for payments to be made on the death of the member whilst in service, but also on death after retirement. This benefit takes various forms; the most usual is a continuing, but usually smaller, widow's or widower's pension. Further particulars of the provisions for survivors' pensions are given below.

10.10 A lump sum payment may also be made. The most common form that this takes is a payment equal to any balance of five years' pension payments, sometimes called a 'pension guarantee'. (This basis applies in the case of about 75 per cent of private sector scheme members and 35 per cent of public sector scheme members.) For about half of public sector scheme members the form that the lump sum takes is the balance (if any) of the benefit that would have been paid on death immediately before retirement over payments already received. In the case of about 20 per cent of private sector and 10 per cent of public sector scheme members no lump sum benefit is payable.

10.11 All public sector schemes provide unconditionally for a widow's pension on the death of a male member after retirement. This is the case for most, but not all, members of private sector schemes, as Table 10.6 shows. For a few members a pension is payable only to a dependent spouse and for others provision is limited to an option to surrender part of the member's own pension at retirement in exchange for a pension payable to a surviving spouse.

Table 10.6 Numbers of male members according to availability of widow's pension on death after retirement

thousands

Availability	Private sector	Public sector	Total
Unconditional	3,830	2,800	6,630
Only if dependent	40	—	40
Only by surrender	130	—	130
No pension	400	—	400
Totals	4,400	2,800	7,200

10.12 In the private sector in 1987 in most schemes widowers of female pensioners were treated in the same way as widows of male pensioners, but it was not until shortly after 1987 that equal treatment in this respect became general in the public sector.

10.13 As in the case of death in service, the spouse's pension on death after retirement is usually based on both salary and service, often being calculated as, say, one-half of the retired employee's pension. Table 10.7 gives the numbers of members according to the mode of calculation and can be compared with the corresponding Table 10.3 for death in service widows' pensions.

Table 10.7 Numbers of male members according to mode of calculation of widow's pension on death after retirement

thousands

Mode of calculation	Private sector	Public sector	Total
From member's salary and service	3,740	2,780	6,520
From either the member's salary or his length of service	50	—	50
From the amount of the member's pension (when that is provided on a money purchase or similar basis)	210	20	230
No widow's pension	400	—	400
Totals	4,400	2,800	7,200

10.14   Table 10.8 gives an indication of the level of widow's pension for those cases where the pension is based on the member's salary and service. Widow's pension benefits in the private sector are generally based upon a higher pension fraction per year of service than those of the public sector. Although part of the member's pension is usually commuted for a lump sum, the widow's pension is based on the member's pension before commutation.

Table 10.8 Numbers of male members in schemes with widow's pension on death after retirement based on salary and service according to pension fraction per year of service

thousands

Fraction	Private sector	Public sector	Total
100ths or better	610	—	610
Between 100ths and 120ths	160	140	300
120ths	2,230	—	2,230
Between 120ths and 160ths	260	—	260
160ths	420	2,640	3,060
Less than 160ths	60	—	60
Totals	3,740	2,780	6,520

Remarriage

10.15   Should a widow remarry it is the normal practice in the public sector for her pension to be suspended or stopped entirely, except for the guaranteed minimum pension required as a condition for contracting out. Table 10.9 shows that about 75 per cent of male members in the private sector and about 20 per cent in the public sector are in schemes where the payment of a widow's pension is unaffected by her remarriage. For the remaining members the pension will often continue at a lower level, but usually only at the minimum rate acceptable for contracting-out purposes. In the private sector the proportion of female members according to whether the widower's pension is affected by his remarriage are similar to those for male members relating to widows' pensions.

Table 10.9   Numbers of male members according to whether the widow's pension is affected by her remarriage

thousands

	Private sector	Public sector	Total
Unaffected by remarriage	3,310	500	3,810
Reduced to minimum or stopped entirely	390	1,580	1,970
May be continued at trustees' discretion	170	370	540
Ceases if remarriage takes place			
before age 60	130	350	480
No widow's pension	400	—	400
Totals	4,400	2,800	7,200

Post-retirement marriages

10.16   In 1975 almost three-quarters of male members in schemes granting unconditional widows' pensions on death after retirement were not covered in respect of marriages contracted after retirement. In 1987 only 20 per cent of all male members were in schemes not providing cover in respect of such marriages and some of those would still be covered for the guaranteed minimum pension. Of the remaining 80 per cent, however, about one-fifth would not be covered (or only covered at the trustees' discretion) if marriage had taken place within six months of death. The figures are set out in Table 10.10.

56

Table 10.10 Numbers of male members' pensions according to whether widows' pensions* are
granted in respect of post-retirement marriages

thousands

Pensions	Private sector	Public sector	Total
Granted	1,840	370	2,210
Granted for service after 1978	310	1,610	1,920
Granted unless marriage occurred			
within 6 months of death	1,110	120	1,230
Not granted post retirement	740	700	1,440
No widows' pensions in scheme	400	—	400
Totals	4,400	2,800	7,200

*Other than the guaranteed minimum pensions required for contracting out.

11 Preservation for Early Leavers

11.1   Employees leaving an occupational pension scheme can now take a refund of their contributions only if they leave within two years of joining, and otherwise their benefits must be preserved or the rights transferred to another scheme or secured through the purchase of an annuity contract with an insurance company. However, at the time the survey was made in 1987 the Social Security Acts only required occupational pension schemes to provide for the preservation of retirement benefits for those leaving a scheme with at least five years' qualifying service. In practice the right to a preserved pension is not always limited to the statutory requirement; in particular, many members who left schemes before the preservation requirement was introduced in 1973 were granted preserved pension rights in the schemes they had left. In total about 3½ million people had preserved rights in 1987. From answers to the General Household Survey it can be deduced that about 2½ million of them were not currently in another scheme. Table 11.1 shows an estimated breakdown of the numbers of these deferred pensioners in detail. It should be noted that the number with preserved rights does not include the cases where benefits earned in a previous employment were all secured through a transfer payment.

11.2   Of the estimated 3½ million deferred pensioners, about 1 million arise from public sector schemes, though for movement between public sector schemes it is usual for a transfer payment to be made.

11.3   For service before 1985 there was no legal requirement for preserved pensions to be increased to allow for inflation. However, schemes which were contracted-out of the earnings-related additional pension under the state scheme and which meet their liability for guaranteed minimum pension in respect of a withdrawing member through a preserved pension in the scheme are required to increase the GMP element on one of three bases as national average earnings

Table 11.1 Number of deferred pensioners

millions

Status	Men	Women	Total
In employment:			
Members of current employer's scheme	0.9	0.2	1.1
Not members of current employer's scheme	0.5	0.3	0.8
Totals in employment	1.4	0.5	1.9
Not in employment:			
Currently self-employed	0.3	0.1	0.4
Economically inactive	0.6	0.6	1.2
Totals of deferred pensioners	2.3	1.2	3.5

rise. Questions were asked in the survey to assess how far schemes were providing increases in preserved pensions in excess of the statutory minima. The results are summarized in Table 11.2.

Table 11.2 Preserved benefits: numbers of members in schemes

millions

Question		Private sector	Public sector	Total
Do preserved benefits include a lump sum or widow's pension on the death of an ex-employee before pension age?				
	YES	4.8	4.8	9.6
	NO	1.0	—	1.0
		5.8	4.8	10.6
Are preserved benefits for pre-1985 service in excess of the guaranteed minimum pension, increased during deferment?				
	YES	3.0	4.7	7.7
	NO	2.8	0.1	2.9
		5.8	4.8	10.6

Increases in preserved pensions

11.4   Table 11.2 shows that in the private sector in 1987 just over half of members are in schemes which made provisions for increasing the preserved pension of early leavers in the period up to normal retirement age, compared with just over 40 per cent in 1983 when the same questions were asked. For about 70 per cent of these members the last increase granted in respect of preserved pensions was less than 5 per cent, with 3 per cent being the most common rate of increase. There were very few cases where increases in preserved pensions were linked to the cost of living. In the public sector preserved pensions have for many years been increased in line with the Retail Prices Index.

Transfer payments

11.5   Under the Social Security Act 1985 schemes became obliged from 1st January 1986 to offer transfer values to all members leaving not later than one year before normal pension age. During the first half of 1987 there were some 65,000 such transfer values paid to another scheme from private sector schemes and 14,000 from public sector schemes (excluding transfer within the local government scheme), together with some 95,000 and 1,300 respectively paid to insurance companies for annuity contracts. For pre-1986 leavers most public sector schemes grant transfer values on request, although a few large schemes grant them in certain circumstances only. The position in respect of private sector scheme members was that 90 per cent of them are members of schemes which grant transfer values to other schemes on request for pre-1986 leavers, but only 70 per cent were at that time in schemes in which the purchase of an annuity contract would be permitted. About 5 per cent of members belonged to schemes which would not allow such transfer payments in any circumstances, and a further 20 per cent are members of schemes where the purchase of an annuity contract would not be permitted.

12 Appointment of Trustees

12.1   Pension schemes other than statutory arrangements are normally required, in order to secure Inland Revenue approval, to be set up as trusts and to be administered by trustees. Previous surveys have asked questions about the form of the trust arrangements but these were not repeated on the present occasion.

12.2   Although all trustees, regardless of the form of the trust or how they are appointed, have a duty to administer a pension scheme in accordance with the trust deed and rules and to ensure that the fund is fairly applied for all the persons entitled to benefit, there has been interest in the manner in which trustees are selected and the extent to which members have a say in the appointments. Questions were asked to establish whether any of the trustees were elected by the members or nominated, by Trade Unions or otherwise, as representing the members. The results for schemes with more than 12 members are shown in Table 12.1. Where some member representatives are elected and some nominated the scheme has been included in the category *elected member(s)* in the table.

Table 12.1 Numbers of schemes and of members according to whether a representative of the employees is a trustee

Status of representative	Private sector		Public sector
	Schemes	Members	Members
		thousands	thousands
Elected member(s)	1,800	1,580	160
Trade union nominated member(s)	500	1,060	370
Other nominated member(s)	6,400	780	220
None elected or nominated	13,500	1,900	50
No trustees	1,300	180	4,000
Totals	23,500	5,500	4,800

12.3   About 60 per cent of members in the private sector are in schemes administered by trustees some at least of whom are elected or nominated as representatives of the members.

Appendix A1   Method of the Survey

Scope of the survey

A1.1   This survey covers the occupational pension schemes (for definition see the glossary at Appendix A3) of employers of all types and sizes of business and other organisations throughout the United Kingdom, and the Armed Forces. It does not, however, cover the pension arrangements of the self-employed and gives relatively little information about schemes which cover only one or two employees.

GHS data on scheme membership

A1.2   The sample for the survey consisted of employees in the 1987 General Household Survey (the GHS), a continuous survey carried out by the Office of Population Censuses and Surveys and based on a sample of the general population resident in private households in Great Britain. Most of the information on private sector pension schemes given in this report is ultimately based on the 1987 GHS sample of 10,275 people in households in Great Britain who said that they were employed either full-time or part-time (excluding students). This linkage with the GHS not only provides a sound statistical basis for the sample and hence a reliable estimate of the number of scheme members, but also opens the possibility of collating information about (anonymous) individuals and the schemes to which they belong. Other sources had to be used for Northern Ireland. In the public sector it was possible to augment GHS data on the number of scheme members with an almost complete coverage by direct enquiries to the major schemes and employers.

A1.3   Table A1.1 summarizes the scheme membership of the 10,080 GHS respondents who were in employment at the date of interview according to their sector and working hours. The 178 respondents for whom the sector or working hours were not known are excluded.

Table A1.1 GHS respondents* according to pension scheme membership

Great Britain, 1987

Status	Men			Women		
	Total respondents	Pension scheme members	Percentage members	Total respondents	Pension scheme members	Percentage members
Private sector:			%			%
Full-time	3,783	1,928	51	1,748	568	32
Part-time	218	15	7	1,397	90	6
Totals	4,001	1,943		3,145	658	
Public sector:						
Full-time	1,315	1,213	92	829	738	89
Part-time	76	9	12	714	148	21
Totals	1,391	1,222		1,543	886	
Both sectors:						
Full-time	5,098	3,141	62	2,577	1,306	51
Part-time	294	24	8	2,111	238	11
Totals	5,392	3,165		4,688	1,544	
Men and women Both sectors:						
Full-time	7,675	4,447				
Part-time	2,405	262				
Totals	10,080	4,709				

* For more details of the scheme membership as it affects the 7,675 full-time employees (5,098 men and 2,577 women) included in the above table see Table 7.4 in the published GHS Report for 1987.

Where the individual had more than one employment the information relates to the main job. The 49 respondents who were recorded as not sure if they were in a scheme but thought it possible are included as members. (This lack of knowledge was sometimes accounted for by the fact that another member of the household was answering for a person who was not present when the interview took place.)

A1.4 The GHS covers private households and hence it does not provide a representative sample for certain groups of the population. In particular, few members of the Armed Forces are in private households and so the GHS respondents who were members of the Armed Forces have been excluded from the main analysis of the GHS data. The numbers of members of the Armed Forces Pension Scheme shown in the tables in the report have been obtained from the Ministry of Defence. Some nurses are also not in private households and this may have had some small effect on the GHS results for public sector women employees. However, a direct count of the membership of nearly all public sector schemes indicates that probably the GHS generally underestimates the coverage of women in public sector schemes. This is particularly likely to be the case in non-contributory schemes, but probably occurs in contributory schemes also, and also in the private sector. In view of this the percentage coverage figures for women employees have been taken as one or two percentage points higher than indicated by the GHS.

A1.5   The GHS does not cover Northern Ireland, but some information has been collected on pension schemes in Northern Ireland. In making the adjustments to the GHS coverage percentages as described above it has been assumed that the same proportion of public sector employees are members of schemes in Northern Ireland as in Great Britain, but that in the private sector the proportion of members is a little lower than in Great Britain because of the different industrial composition of the work force. The total number of members of occupational pension schemes who are employed in Northern Ireland is estimated at about 200,000, or 2 per cent of the total for the United Kingdom.

A1.6   The estimated coverage percentages are applied to numbers of employees in employment in 1987 obtained from the *Labour Force Survey* for Great Britain (see Bibliography), adjusted to cover the whole of the United Kingdom. To be in accord with the GHS definition of an employee the figures extracted from the LFS were those which avoided the double-counting of employees with more than one employment. The results are shown in Table A1.2. In view of the various possible errors in the information used the resulting membership estimates for the male and female members in each sector have been rounded to the nearest 100,000 and the total membership is as a result given as a round figure of 10,600,000 persons.

Table A1.2 Calculation of numbers of men and women in schemes

Status	Employees in employment	Assumed percentage membership	Employees in schemes
	thousands	%	thousands
Men:			
Full-time			
Private sector	8,500	51	4,370
Public sector	2,700	92	2,490
Part-time			
Private sector	400	7	30
Public sector	100	12	10
HM Forces	300	98	300
Totals	12,000	60	7,200
Women:			
Full-time			
Private sector	3,400	34	1,200
Public sector	1,900	91	1,700
Part-time			
Private sector	2,900	7	200
Public sector	1,400	21	300
HM Forces	20	98	20
Totals	9,600	35	3,400
Men and women:			
Totals	21,600	49	10,600

The Government Actuary's questionnaire

A1.7   The main objective of the Government Actuary's surveys has always been to collect detailed information about pension schemes, and this information can in practice only be reliably obtained from scheme managers or employers. Thus a special 'follow-up' sheet was completed at the end of the GHS interview for as many as possible of the GHS respondents who said that they were, or might be, a member of a scheme in order to obtain the name or address of their pension scheme. ('Proxies', ie those answering the GHS questions in place of another member of the household, were *not* asked for this information.) Sheets were completed for 4,442 of the 4,811 respondents who said that they were or might be in a scheme and, of the 4,442 completed sheets, 2,414 were for respondents in the private sector. The Government Actuary's Department (GAD) was normally provided with the name and address of the scheme or of the employer, to whom a six-page questionnaire (see Appendix A2) could be sent. Often more than one GHS respondent was in a particular scheme, so reducing the number of employers that needed to be approached. Small private sector schemes run by employers were approached only on the basis of the GHS sample; however, all the main public sector schemes were approached, whether sampled by the GHS or not, as were all large private sector schemes. It was emphasized that all information received would be treated in confidence by the Government Actuary's Department and that no information relating to individual schemes would be disclosed.

A1.8   In 10 cases, mainly because of the lack of an adequate address, it was not possible for a questionnaire to be sent. In addition, although GAD was normally given the follow-up sheet (which was completed by the GHS interviewer) to process, no information was given to GAD which would enable anyone in that department to discover the identity of any respondent, thus protecting the confidentiality of respondents of the GHS. To ensure this confidentiality, GHS staff (and not GAD) sent out the questionnaire to (and received it back from) 138 GHS respondents who were themselves the scheme manager.

A1.9   Table A1.3 shows the numbers of GHS private sector scheme members who gave usable addresses for their scheme managers classified according to whether their manager responded or did not respond to the questionnaire. The response rate of 75 per cent was high for a postal survey of this nature and exceeded the level of 72 per cent achieved in the 1983 survey. The table also shows an estimate of the numbers of different employers involved.

Table A1.3   GHS private sector respondents for whom a follow-up sheet was available

	Employers	Hits	
Responders	975	1,813	(75%)
Non-responders	425	591	(25%)
Totals	1,400	2,404	(100%)

A1.10   In order to obtain earlier replies and to increase the coverage of the sample, 768 large private sector schemes identified from the publication *Pension Funds and their Advisers 1987* (PFA) as having, or being likely to have, over 1000 members were sent a questionnaire at the outset of the survey. Many, but not all, of the schemes involved were eventually hit by the GHS, so that the total number of private sector schemes approached (1,395) was somewhat greater than the number that would have been approached on the basis of GHS hits alone. At the same time, most of the larger British pension schemes had more than one GHS respondent who was a member and so the number of different schemes involved as far as the GHS sample was concerned was far fewer than the total number of GHS respondents who were members of schemes. The outcome of the private sector sampling is shown in Table A1.3. This is expressed in terms of numbers of individual employers, many of whom have more than one scheme in force.

Private sector rating-up factors for the United Kingdom

A1.11   The next stage in the production of the total numbers of scheme members entitled to various levels of benefit etc was to rate up the answers on the individual questionnaires. In principle, as there were 2,266 'hits' of private sector employees in schemes and there were reckoned to be 5,800,000 members, each hit could have been reckoned to represent 2,560 members. However, as Table A1.3 shows, replies were obtained for only 1,813 hits, ie 75 per cent of cases. Each of the 1,813 cases in which a response was obtained could have been taken to represent 3,199 members, but, because the proportion of small schemes responding by completing a questionnaire was relatively low, this would have resulted in a bias in the results towards the characteristics of the larger schemes. In addition it would not have made use of the data obtained from those larger schemes which had been approached and had completed a questionnaire, but whose members had not been among those hit by the GHS.

A1.12   Thus rating-up factors were calculated according to the size of scheme as reported on the questionnaire by using a formula incorporating the probability of non-response and the probability of having a GHS respondent among its membership, adjusted to take account of schemes without a GHS respondent who completed a questionnaire. Table A1.4 shows the rating-up factor for various sizes of schemes for those schemes for which a completed questionnaire was received. Thus, for example, a questionnaire reporting a scheme with 300 members is taken to represent 13 similar schemes, with a total membership of 3,900 persons.

Table A1.4 Rating-up factors for private sector schemes of various sizes

Actual scheme size (members)	Rating-up factor	Rated-up weight of scheme (members)
100,000	1.10	110,000
10,000	1.22	12,200
1,000	2.72	2,720
300	13	3,900
100	46	4,600
30	172	5,160
10	581	5,810
3	2,262	6,786
1	8,014	8,014

A1.13   The results for schemes with up to 12 members must be treated with some caution, not only because there is likely to be some doubt as to whether an arrangement for 1 to 3 people constitutes a scheme or not, but also because they depend on a sample of only about 125 GHS respondents, with a relatively low response rate in terms of their completion of the pension scheme survey questionnaire. However, in the context of the overall picture of the scope and coverage of occupational schemes, the small sample of schemes with 12 or fewer members is not a major drawback as such schemes represent under 5 per cent of the total membership of schemes in the private sector.

Public sector scheme membership

A1.14   The direct survey of public sector schemes by GAD, covering the whole of the United Kingdom, shows an estimated total civilian membership of 4,560,000. This total comprises about 4,200,000 full-time and 300,000 part-time public sector employees, together with 65,000 private sector employees, such as teachers in independent schools participating in the national teachers' pensions scheme. These figures are based on an analysis of both the returned questionnaires and data from other government sources. In addition there are 320,000 members in the Armed Forces. Thus, excluding the private sector employees, there are reckoned to be, in round numbers, 4.8 million public sector employees in pension schemes.

A1.15   Questions were returned from schemes, or information obtained from other government sources, covering 97.5 per cent of the total public sector civilian membership, and in the limited areas where full data were not obtained estimates were made to allow for the missing schemes.

Financial questions

A1.16   To meet a need for information about the income and expenditure of pension schemes (which was not included in the main questionnaire on this occasion) separate supplementary questionnaires asking for financial information were sent to pension schemes some months after the main questionnaires. The results are reported in Chapter 4.

Appendix A2   Copies of Questionnaires

(i) Main questionnaire

(ii) Financial questions questionnaire

OCCUPATIONAL PENSION SCHEMES 1987

Eighth Survey by the Government Actuary

Confidential

Any information given will be treated in confidence by the Government Actuary and no information relating to individual schemes will be disclosed.

Queries about the completion of the form should be addressed to the Government Actuary's Department, 22 Kingsway, London WC2B 6LE. Telephone enquiries may be made to 01-242 6828.

Employees outside the United Kingdom and all matters relating to them or their pensions should be excluded.

Approximate answers should be given if the exact figures cannot be obtained.

Schemes providing only lump sums on retirement, or only widows' pensions, should be included, but not those providing only a lump sum on death.

1 a **Name and address of scheme**

b or, if you have no retirement or widows' benefit scheme for the employees indicated in the letter, put a tick in the box and return the form.

No scheme ☐

Ring the numbers applicable

c Name and telephone number of the person to whom any further enquiries should be addressed

d Is the scheme open to new members?   1 Yes   2 No

2 Which employees are covered by the scheme?

Works or manual employees	1
Staff or non-manual employees	2
Senior executives or management	3

Active members are those currently employed

3 Number of active members in June 1987

	Men	Women	Total
Full-time	....	....	....
Part-time	....	....	....
Total	....	....	....

Part-time preferably means employed for less than 31 hours a week

4 Numbers of all pensions and preserved benefits in 1987

A preserved benefit is a pension or lump sum promised to an ex-employee which will be paid at retirement age

	Former male employees	Former female employees	Widow(er)s and dependants
Number of pensions in payment in June 1987	....	....	....
Number of preserved benefits promised, but not yet in payment	....	....	

5 Contracting out

a Is the scheme a contracted-out scheme for the purposes of the state pension scheme?   1 Yes   2 No

b If yes, how many members are not covered by the contracting-out certificate?

Men	Women
....	....

74

6 At what minimum age can employees join the scheme?

No minimum age (or age 16)	1	
At age	2	years
Discretionary	3	

7 What minimum period of service do employees have to complete before joining the scheme?

No minimum	1	
Less than 1 year	2	
Period of 1 year or more; give number	3	years
Other (please give details)	4	

Give the percentages for the main groups of members

8 How do members contribute?

No contribution	1	
Compulsory level percentage of pay or pensionable pay	2	%
Other basis (please describe)	3	
Is pensionable pay for contributions purposes less than actual pay to allow for state scheme contributions or benefits?	1 yes 2 no 3 not applicable	

9 Integration with state pensions

a Are the earnings used for calculating benefits reduced to allow for the state pension? 1 yes 2 no

b If yes, what form(s) does the reduction take?

Pay for pension scheme purposes is reduced by an amount depending on the basic state pension or the lower earnings limit	1
Pay for pension scheme purposes is reduced by a fixed amount	2
Pensionable pay is not reduced, but the pension is reduced by an amount related to the basic state pension	3
Pension is reduced by applying different pension accrual fractions to different bands of pay or by the amount of the state earnings-related pension	4
Other methods are used	5

10 What are the normal retirement ages under the rules?

Men   Women

. . . .

In this question any reduction for integration with the state scheme should be disregarded

11 What are the benefits at normal retirement age?

Pension that is a fraction of pay for each year's service: give fraction . . .   1

$1/$

. . . and the period over which the earnings are taken or averaged

. . . and whether these earnings are revalued to allow for inflation

If some members' benefits differ from others, plese describe

Pension on some other basis (please describe: eg money purchase) in which case give the level of the employer's contributions   2

Lump sum other than by commutation of pension (please describe)   3

12 Are the following fluctuating items included in pay when calculating pensions?

Bonuses   1 yes 2 no
3 not applicable

Overtime payments   1 yes 2 no
3 not applicable

Commission   1 yes 2 no
3 not applicable

13 What is the benefit on early retirement due to ill health?

No immediate benefit   1

Accrued pension reduced because of early payment   2

Accrued pension unreduced   3

Unreduced accrued pension plus part of future potential pension   4

Unreduced accrued pension plus the whole of the future potential pension   5

Benefit from a Permanent Health Insurance scheme   6

A minimum of a certain percentage of salary (please give details)   7

Other benefit (please specify)   8

14 Other early retirement

a Are pensions paid from the pension fund immediately on early retirement when retirement is not on grounds of ill health?

Not in any circumstances	1
Only on the initiative of the member	2
Only on the initiative of the employer	3
On the initiative of either the member or the employer	4

b When early retirement is on the initiative of the *member* what criteria have to be satisfied by the member with regard to minimum age and length of service?

c When early retirement is on the initiative of the *employer*

(i) what criteria have to be satisfied by the member with regard to minimum age and length of service?

(ii) what do the rules of the scheme state that the minimum pension granted is to be?

accrued pension reduced by normal actuarial factors	1
accrued pension reduced by specially favourable actuarial factors or additional service counted	2
accrued pension, unreduced	3
at the employer's discretion, or not stated in rules	4

---

15 Benefits on death in service

	Male member	Female member
a What benefits are payable on death in service?		
No benefit	1	1
Lump sum and/or return of contributions (Please describe basis and state any difference according to marital status)	2	2
A pension to the surviving spouse	3	3

b If a surviving spouse's pension is payable how is it related to the member's salary or potential pension?

	Widows	Widowers
. . . and, is it payable in all cases in which there is a surviving spouse?	1 yes 2 no	1 yes 2 no
. . . is it payable only where the spouse was dependent on the member?	1 yes 2 no	1 yes 2 no
. . . or is it payable only if the member exercised an option?	1 yes 2 no	1 yes 2 no

16 Benefits on death after retirement

		Male member	Female member
a	What benefits can be paid?		
	No benefit	1	1
	Lump sum or balance of member's contributions (please describe basis)	2	2
	Spouse's pension in all cases where there is a surviving spouse (please describe how the spouse's pension is related to the member's pension)	3	3
	Spouse's pension only if the member had exercised an option (eg by allocation)	4	4
	Spouse's pension only where the spouse was dependent on the member	5	5
b	How is a spouse's pension (if any) on death after retirement affected by remarriage?		
	Always reduced or stopped	1	1
	Discretionary whether reduced or stopped	2	2
	Ceases only if remarriage before a particular age (eg age 60)	3	3
	Not affected by remarriage	4	4
c	Are spouse's pensions granted in respect of post-retirement marriages?		
	Always	1	
	For service after 1978 only	2	
	Yes, except for marriage within 6 months of death	3	
	Never	4	

Spouse's pension means widow's or widower's pension as the case may be

17 Increases in pensions in payment

If different percentages apply to different members please describe

a By what percentage were pensions in payment increased

in 1984?	%
in 1985?	%
in 1986?	%

b Is the pension reduced for any reason when calculating the increase applicable?

GMP is the guaranteed minimum pension under the state pension scheme

no	1
by the GMP	2
by any other amount	3
not applicable	4

c What increase (if any) is required by the rules of the scheme?   %

A preserved benefit is a pension or lump sum promised to an ex-employee which will be paid at retirement age (or, possibly, on earlier death)

18 Preserved benefits

	Male member	Female member
a Do preserved benefits include a lump sum or spouse's pension on the death of the ex-employee before pension age?	1 yes 2 no	1 yes 2 no
b Are preserved benefits for service before 1985 that are in excess of the guaranteed minimum pension, if any, increased during deferment?	1 yes 2 no	

If so, please give details of the most recent increase

19 Trustees (If the answer to question 19a is 'no' proceed to question 20)

a Are there any trustees? — 1 yes 2 no

b If there are trustees, are they only the employer or group of employers (or a company or body acting for them)? — 1 yes 2 no

Are any of the trustees individuals elected by the scheme members? — 1 yes 2 no

Are any of the trustees individuals nominated by Trade Unions? — 1 yes 2 no

Are any of them otherwise nominated (eg by the employer) as representatives of scheme members? — 1 yes 2 no

20 Transfer values

a How many payments of transfer values were made between 1 January 1987 and 30 June 1987 to

(i) other occupational pension schemes?

(ii) insurance companies for annuity contracts?

b In what circumstances do scheme members who left *before* 1 January 1986 now have a right to

(i) transfer pension rights to another scheme?

On request — 1

Only in certain circumstances — 2

Not at all — 3

(ii) use their pension rights to buy an annuity contract from an insurance company?

On request — 1

Only in certain circumstances — 2

Not at all — 3

Thank you for your time and co-operation

Financial questions questionnaire

The response should cover a 12-month period which ended between April 1987 and March 1988

Include under employer's contributions special contributions and any expenditure on supplementary pension payments met directly by the employer. (These should also appear under pension expenditure.)

Gross means including tax credits, but irrecoverable overseas withholding tax should be deducted, as should other outgoings in respect of investments (eg ground rent).

Exclude capital items such as realized or unrealized profits on investments.

Include with pensions or other benefits (including refunds to employees or to employers) any income tax deducted from these payments and paid to the Inland Revenue.

Exclude premiums for permanent disability benefits unless the benefits are included in the receipts from insurance companies shown above.

Exclude capital items such as realized or unrealized losses on investments.

Exclude funds held by insurance companies (unless the underlying assets are registered in the names of the trustees of the schemes).

Period	from	to

Income £

Employer's contributions and premiums _____

Members' contributions (excluding next item below) _____

Additional voluntary contributions _____

Transfer payments from other pension schemes _____

Gross rent, dividends, interest and other investment income _____

Receipts from life insurance companies (if any) _____

Miscellaneous income _____

Total income _____

Expenditure £

Pensions paid to former employees _____

Pensions paid to widow(er)s and dependants of former employees _____

Lump sums on death _____

Lump sums on retirement _____

Transfer payments to other pension arrangements _____

State scheme premiums _____

Refunds to employers _____

Refunds to employees _____

Expenses met from fund _____

Payments (eg premiums) to life insurance companies _____

Miscellaneous expenditure _____

Total expenditure _____

Market value of funds £

What was the market value of the funds at the end of the period (net assets)? _____

Appendix A3   Glossary

Many of the definitions below are derived from Pensions Terminology *published by the PMI (see Bibliography, Appendix A4) and are copyright.*

Accrued pension
The pension to which a member is entitled for service up to a given point in time, whether the member leaves service then or not.

Additional voluntary contributions
Contributions over and above a member's normal contributions (if any) which a member elects to pay in order to secure additional benefits.

Allocation
The giving up (usually of part) of a pension by one person in return for a pension or contingent pension to another (for instance a widow).

Assets
The property, investments, debtors, cash and other items to which a body such as an insurance company or the *trustees* of a pension fund have title.

Average earnings scheme
A scheme where the benefit for each year of membership is related to the pensionable earnings for that year.

Central government
Employers in the central government of the economy as defined for national accounts purposes. The sector not only includes government departments and the Armed Forces but a number of publicly constituted boards and the like which are effectively controlled by the government in major matters such as employees' pension arrangements. Important examples are the Health Authorities, the Atomic Energy Authority, the Forestry Commission and the Medical Research Council.

Centralized scheme
A scheme operated on behalf of several employers, but usually only covering one industry (for instance the building trade or social workers).

Closed scheme
A scheme which does not admit new members, but still has employees contributing to it or pensions paid from it.

Commutation
The giving up of a part or all of the pension payable from retirement in return for an immediate cash sum.

Contracting out
To use the statutory arrangement under which, in return for lower state scheme contributions, members of occupational pension schemes that meet certain conditions may be excluded from the main part of additional earnings-related benefits under the state scheme. The occupational scheme takes responsibility for providing a corresponding *guaranteed minimum pension* instead (except under *money purchase schemes* which have become eligible for contracting out only since the time of this survey).

Coverage
The proportion of the number of members of an occupational pension scheme to the number of employees from whom the members are drawn.

Current scheme
A scheme giving benefits in respect of current employment.

Deferred pension
A pension whose commencement is postponed beyond the normal retiring age. (Should not be used as meaning *preserved pension*.)

Deferred pensioner
Usually, a person who has a *preserved* pension.

Dependant
Any person who is financially dependent on a pension scheme member or pensioner, or was so at the time of death of the member or pensioner.

Discretionary pensions increase
An increase in pensions in payment (or preserved benefits) other than in accordance with a formula specified in the rules of the scheme.

Employees, and full-time or part-time employment
In the aggregate, employees in employment, as defined by the Department of Employment, together with HM Forces, but with no person counted more than once. The self-employed, home workers and private domestic servants are excluded, and part-time employees without another job are counted as one person, rather than a fraction of an employee.

Part-time employees are those who work for 30 hours or less per week, excluding overtime (but 25 hours or less for teachers and lecturers).

Employer
The person or body with whom a person has a contract of employment, except that in this report a group of employers having a common pension scheme is treated as a single employer.

Enhancement
Increase of length of *pensionable service* beyond that actually completed.

Establishment, size of
The number of employees working at the place of employment, as stated by an employee to a *GHS* interviewer.

Final-salary pension scheme
A scheme in which the benefit is calculated by reference to *pensionable salary* for a period ending at, or not long before, retirement.

Flat-rate pension
A pension of a fixed amount, for example £10 a year for each year's membership of the scheme irrespective of earnings.

Funded scheme
A scheme in which benefits are met from a fund built up in advance from contributions and investment income.

General government sector
Employees in the *central government* and *local authority* sectors of the economy as defined for national accounts purposes.

General Household Survey (GHS)
A continuous survey, with a questionnaire changed annually, carried out by the Office of Population Censuses and Surveys and based on a sample of the population resident in households in Great Britain.

Group pension scheme business
Business described as such by insurance companies in their returns to the Department of Trade and Industry, representing their pension scheme business for groups of employees.

Guaranteed minimum pension (GMP)
The minimum pension which, at the time of this survey, all occupational schemes had to provide as one of the conditions for *contracting out*.

Guaranteed pension
An arrangement whereby on the early death of a pensioner the pension scheme pays a further sum or sums to meet a guaranteed total.

Indexation, index linking or inflation proofing
A system whereby pensions in payment and/or preserved benefits are automatically increased at regular intervals by reference to changes in a specified index of prices (or earnings).

Insured scheme
A pension scheme under which the benefits are provided wholly or partly by means of a contract with an insurance company (including a *managed fund* contract).

Local authorities
Employers in the sector of the economy as defined for national accounts purposes which consists of the public authorities of limited geographic scope, having power to raise funds by certain forms of taxation. They include county, borough, district and parish councils, and joint boards and committees formed by two or more councils.

Managed fund
An insurance contract by means of which an insurance company offers investment through participation in one or more pooled funds.

Member of a pension scheme
In this report the persons currently employed who are entitled to benefits in respect of their current employment.

Money purchase scheme
A pension scheme in which the benefits for an individual member are directly determined by the amount of contributions paid into the scheme in respect of that member, increased by an amount based on the investment return on those contributions.

Non-contributory scheme
A scheme in which no contributions are required from members, either as a general rule, or as a result of a temporary suspension applying at the time of the survey.

Normal retirement age
The age specified in the rules of a scheme at which the members normally retire and can receive an unreduced pension based on their *pensionable service*.

Notionally funded
The schemes for teachers, for the National Health Service and for the Atomic Energy Authority which have no actual investments but which for the purpose of assessing contribution rates are deemed to purchase investments and receive an income from them. They are treated in the same way as *unfunded schemes* for the purpose of the accounts in this survey, as if income exactly balanced outgo.

Occupational pension scheme
An arrangement (other than accident or permanent health insurance) organized by an employer (or on behalf of a group of employers) to provide benefits for employees on their retirement and for their dependants on their death. In this survey the term is extended to include schemes providing a lump sum on retirement which the employee is free to convert into a pension if desired.

Part-time employee
See under *employee*.

Pension fraction
The fraction of *pensionable salary* for each year of *pensionable service* which forms the basis of the pension in a *final-salary pension scheme*.

Pensionable salary
The amount of salary on which benefits are calculated. It may exclude a fixed amount of earnings or overtime, commission and similar payments.

Pensionable service
The period of service with an employer which is taken into account in calculating the pension benefit.

Permanent Health Insurance
Insurance policies which provide an income until a normal retirement age if a person is unable to work due to long term ill health.

Post retirement pensions increases
Awards of increases in pensions already in payment, usually to compensate for the fall in value of pensions because of inflation.

Potential service
The amount of service a member would have completed by the *normal retirement age* if death or ill-health retirement had not intervened.

Preservation, preserved benefits
Benefits arising on termination of employment or of scheme membership, the right to which is preserved until *normal retirement age* is reached.

Private sector
Employers not in the *public sector* of the economy as defined for national accounts purposes. Includes some largely independent non-profit making bodies such as the universities.

Public corporations
Employees of the sector of the economy as defined for national accounts purposes which consists of public trading bodies, including the nationalized industries, which have a substantial degree of financial independence from the public authority which created them, including the powers to borrow and maintain reserves. A list of these bodies appears in *United Kingdom National Accounts; Sources and Methods* (see Bibliography). Within limits they have the responsibility to make their own pension arrangements for their employees.

Public sector
Employees in the *central government, local authority* and *public corporation* sectors of the economy as defined for national accounts purposes.

Qualifying service
The period of service, now two years, which must be completed before a right to *preserved benefits* under the Social Security Acts is established; also used in other contexts as the service qualifying for benefit or for admission to a scheme.

Retail Prices Index (RPI)
The official General Index of Retail Prices which is published monthly in the *Employment Gazette*.

Scheme anniversary
Fixed date (usually once a year) on which entry to certain schemes is deemed to take place.

Self-administered scheme

A pension scheme in which the assets are invested by the trustees or an internal or external investment manager, rather than through an insurance contract with an insurance company.

Senior staff scheme

A scheme covering senior executives or management employees only. The employer may have another scheme for other employees.

Staff employees scheme

A scheme covering staff or non-manual employees only, and usually covering only employees in management, professional, administrative, selling or office employment.

Surrender of pension

The giving up (usually of part) of a pension by one person in return for a pension or contingent pension to another (for instance a widow). Also described as *allocation*. See also *commutation*.

Transfer payment

A payment made by one scheme to another when a member changes employment to enable the receiving scheme to give benefits in lieu of the benefit rights which had accrued in the transferring scheme, as an alternative to *preservation*.

Trustees

For most schemes, which are set up as trusts, the body of persons (or the company) appointed to administer the scheme in accordance with the trust deed and rules.

Unfunded scheme

A scheme in which no fund is built up to provide in advance for pensions and other benefits (except possibly a *notional fund*).

Waiting period

Period of service specified in the rules which the employee must serve before being entitled to join a pension scheme or, having joined, to receive a particular benefit.

Works employees scheme

A scheme covering works or manual employees only, but may just include those **employ**ees who are paid weekly.

Appendix A4   Bibliography

Regular publications

Occupational Pension Schemes: A Survey by the Government Actuary. HMSO. 1958.

Occupational Pension Schemes: A New Survey by the Government Actuary. HMSO. 1966.

Occupational Pension Schemes: Third Survey by the Government Actuary. HMSO. 1968.

Occupational Pension Schemes: Fourth Survey by the Government Actuary: 1971. HMSO. 1972.

Occupational Pension Schemes: Fifth Survey by the Government Actuary: 1975. HMSO. 1978.

Occupational Pension Schemes: Sixth Survey by the Government Actuary: 1979. HMSO. 1981.

Occupational Pension Schemes: Seventh Survey by the Government Actuary: 1983. HMSO. 1986.

Business Monitor MQ5. Central Statistical Office. Quarterly.

Employment Gazette. Department of Employment. HMSO. Monthly.

Family Expenditure Survey. Department of Employment. HMSO.

Financial Statistics. Central Statistical Office. HMSO. Monthly.

General Household Survey 1987. Office of Population Censuses and Surveys. HMSO. 1989.

Inland Revenue Statistics. Board of Inland Revenue. HMSO.

Insurance Statistics. Association of British Insurers.

Labour Force Survey. Office of Population Censuses and Surveys. HMSO.

Pension Funds and their Advisers. AP Information Services Ltd. Annually.

Survey of Occupational Pension Schemes. The National Association of Pension Funds. Annually.

United Kingdom National Accounts. "The Blue Book". Central Statistical Office. HMSO.

Other publications

Pensions Terminology. Pensions Management Institute. 1988.

Report of the Phillips Committee on the Economic and Financial Problems for the Provisions for Old Age. Cmd.9333. HMSO. 1955.

United Kingdom National Accounts: Sources and Methods. Third Edition. (Studies in Official Statistics No. 37.) HMSO. 1985.

Index

Printed in the United Kingdom for HMSO
Dd 292022 3/91 C21